Kaja *and* Kelod
Balinese Dance in Transition

Sang Hyang Dedari, Bona. A dancer enters trance.
(Courtesy Danielle Toth)

Kaja *and* Kelod
Balinese Dance in
Transition

I Madé Bandem
and
Fredrik Eugene deBoer

Kuala Lumpur
OXFORD UNIVERSITY PRESS
Oxford New York Melbourne
1981

Oxford University Press
Oxford London Glasgow
New York Toronto Melbourne Auckland
Kuala Lumpur Singapore Hong Kong Tokyo
Delhi Bombay Calcutta Madras Karachi
Nairobi Dar es Salaam Cape Town
and associate companies in
Beirut Berlin Ibadan Mexico City

ISBN 0 19 580469 4

Printed in Singapore by Koon Wah Printing (Pte) Ltd.
Published by Oxford University Press, 3, Jalan 13/3,
Petaling Jaya, Selangor, Malaysia

This book is dedicated to the memory of
I Madé Kredek, dancer,
1907—1979

'This dazzling ensemble full of explosions, flights, secret streams, detours in every direction of both internal and external perception, composes a sovereign idea of the theatre, as it has been preserved for us down through the centuries in order to teach us what the theatre never should have ceased to be.'

from Antonin Artaud 'On the Balinese Theatre'
in *The Theatre and its Double*
(New York: Grove Press, p. 59)

Preface

THIS volume is intended to present an overview of the Balinese dance today, with background information and some conceptual apparatus helpful to understanding the subject. In our discussion we seek to bring together traditional Balinese and contemporary Western ways of approaching the arts of performance. We address a general audience interested in learning about the fascinating and beautiful dances of Bali rather than the specialist, but we hope the reader will already have had the opportunity to become acquainted with the basic aspects of the traditional Balinese culture. In the past, writers on Balinese dance had to assume that their readers might never see the dances under discussion, and they therefore devoted a substantial proportion of their accounts to pages of description and evocation so that the reader might get a feeling for the subject as well as an understanding of it. In recent years, however, many troupes of Balinese dancers have toured the world, and a growing number of films and videotapes have been produced in which the dances themselves can be seen; we hope the reader will have access to such opportunities for seeing Balinese dance, or, best of all, will be able to visit Bali and see the dance there in its appropriate context.

Our plan of arrangement is to move from the dances which are correctly performed in or emanate from the most sacred spaces of the island, through genres of lesser sanctity performed in semi-sacred spaces, to dances of a secular nature performed in essentially secular spaces. We then discuss some 'demonic' performances given in ritually dangerous spaces, and finally some tourist performances, perhaps most dangerous of all for the Balinese dance in the long term, are discussed in the epilogue.

Fundamental to understanding the spatial premise on which the arrangement of our book depends is an old Balinese system of directional orientation, the *kaja* to *kelod* axis. 'Kaja' in Balinese means 'toward the mountain', while 'kelod' means 'toward the ocean'. In Balinese tradition the gods have permanent dwelling places on the heights of the mountains, especially on the great central volcano Gunung Agung. Bali's most sacred shrine, Pura Besakih, is located high on the flank of this enormous peak. The area beneath the mountain, the middle world, is considered to be the appropriate place for human beings, while the lowest level, the sea, is habitation for demons and devils. In the ancient Balinese system, the direction kaja leads toward the sacred, the divine, the good. Kelod leads toward the demonic, the chthonic, the evil. The middle world alone is secular space, uncharged with special spiritual forces.

To move from kaja to kelod at the scale of the macro-cosmos is to go from Siwaloka, the highest heaven, by way of the world, to Yamaloka, or hell. At the all-Bali level, to go from kaja to kelod is to go from the top of Gunung Agung to the southern sea, by way of the inhabited land between them. At the village level, it is to go from the most sacred shrine in the inner temple courtyard to the crossroad, the haunted place, and graveyard. In the household compound it is to go from the family shrine enclosure toward the refuse pit. The progression is from the sacred to the demonic by way of the secular. All important spaces and buildings on the island are (or should be) laid out in proper alignment on the kaja-secular-kelod axis.

We wish to express our sincere thanks to all those who have made this work possible, especially to our many Balinese informants, who are too numerous to mention individually. We must, however, invoke the names of a special few of them, great masters of the subject: I Ketut Rindha, Blahbatuh village, Gianyar Province; the late I Madé Kredek, Singapadu, Gianyar; the late I Gusti Bagus Sugriwa, Bungkulan, Buleleng; I Madé Sidja, Bona, Gianyar; and I Nyoman Rembang, Sesetan, Bandung. We wish to thank also the JDR IIIrd Fund and its director, Mr Richard Lanier, for helping to make this collaboration possible. Our sincere thanks are also due to John Emigh, Richard Schechner, and Hildred Geertz, who kindly read our manuscript and commented on it; we are grateful for their penetrating observations and helpful suggestions, although we have not always followed their advice. We also wish to gratefully acknowledge technical consultation on musical matters from Andrew Toth, and we wish to thank Danielle Toth for making available several valuable photographs. Responsibility for errors, however, is entirely our own. Unless otherwise attributed, our work is based on interviews with Balinese authorities and on field research by the authors.

Middletown
Connecticut
June 1979

I MADÉ BANDEM
FREDRIK EUGENE DEBOER

Contents

CONTENTS

Figures

Black and White Plates

Colour Plates

1 Dances of the Inner Temple

THE genres considered in this chapter belong to the most sacred (*wali*) category of Balinese performing arts.[1] They all appear to be of indigenous origin, although later Hindu-Javanese elements can be seen in them as well as the characteristic poses, gestures, and phrases of movement which make up the fundamental vocabulary of movement of Balinese dance. All of these forms belong to what might be called the communal, village-centred aspect of Balinese culture and involve a strong element of audience participation; the degree of training and basic talent required of the performers are low by Balinese standards. Aesthetic factors, however, are important in some of them. In *Gabor*, for example, the skill of the dancers is as important as the beauty of the offerings presented.[2]

Trance is often present in these genres, and with it there is the presumption of possession by divine, or occasionally demonic, spirits. Wali dances are performed in connection with religious rituals, and they are often given in the context of the elaborate schedule of festivals of the Hindu-Balinese religious calendar. Some of them are specifically associated with the old-fashioned Bali Aga villages, in which many very old Balinese traditions and practices have been maintained, while others are found in villages throughout the island.

The wali dances are customarily performed in or originate from the sacred inner temple courtyard, or *jeroan*. This is the most sacred temple space, the inner sanctum. The essential form of the modern Balinese temple is thought by many authorities to be of indigenous origin, dating back to the Neolithic culture of ancestor worshipping Malayo-Polynesian people, who migrated to Bali from the South-East Asian mainland between 2500 and 1000 B.C. These progenitors of the modern Balinese are thought to have already believed that the spirits of departing ancestors went to dwell on the top of the mountain peaks to the north of Bali's fertile southern heartland. From these peaks, and especially from the tallest, Gunung Agung, came the waters necessary to cultivate rice, and from their dwelling places on the peaks the gods also came periodically to visit the realm of human beings below. The visiting gods were received in ter-

[1]

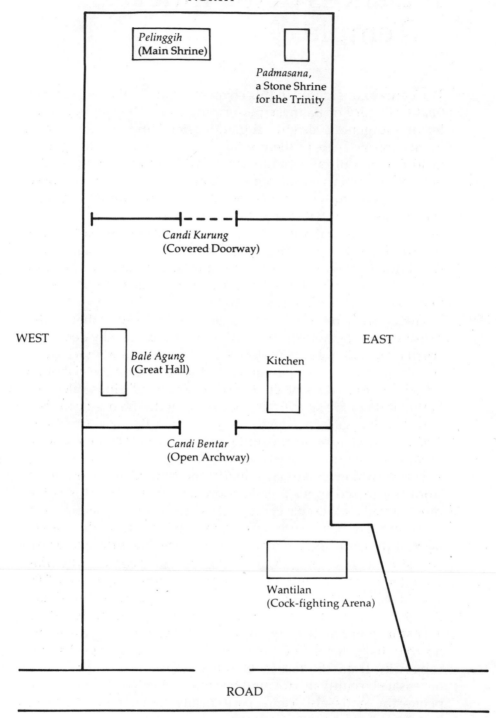

NORTH

Pelinggih
(Main Shrine)

Padmasana,
a Stone Shrine
for the Trinity

Candi Kurung
(Covered Doorway)

WEST

EAST

Balé Agung
(Great Hall)

Kitchen

Candi Bentar
(Open Archway)

Wantilan
(Cock-fighting Arena)

ROAD

SOUTH

1. Plan of a Balinese Temple

raced temples at special times of the year. According to the Dutch archaeologist, Stutterheim, the temples were ringed by a wall to set apart the consecrated area, and they were paved with stones to mark a sacred dancing place before the shrine of the gods. The modern Balinese temple serves similar functions.[3]

Berutuk

In the northern mountain region of Bali, on the shore of Lake Batur in the province of Bangli, stands the ancient village of Trunyan, a Bali Aga village in which many traces of Bali's ancient past are preserved. Near the lake stands the old temple Pura Pancering Jagat ('the Navel of the World'), which is a shrine of modest proportions situated in the shade of an enormous sacred Banyan tree. The temple covers an excavated pit, several yards deep. In the pit stands a large statue of a naked man, about twelve feet tall. His face is rudely carved and fierce of aspect; his arms hang loose at his side; his genitals are large and prominent, though flaccid. This is His Lordship, Dewa Ratu Gedé; only males may enter his presence, and out of respect to him they must be entirely naked when they approach. None may look boldly at him, and all who come near make appropriate gestures of respect.[4]

Every few years, the annual *Odalan*, or regular calendrical festival, in honour of this god becomes the occasion for as strange and interesting a ritual dance-drama as is known in Bali—the dance of the *Berutuk*. Performances are seldom given and at unpredictable intervals, for any uncleanness (*sebel*) in the village, such as an epidemic, a crop failure, or even a death, will be reason for the ceremony to be cancelled. Recent performances were given in 1969 and 1976. It has not yet been determined when the next one will be held.

Performers of the rite are drawn from the *Seka Taruna*, an association of the young bachelors of the village. Their number varies, depending on how many are eligible in the chosen year, but always an odd number of young men participate. There are twenty-one masks available, and that is the maximum possible

[3]

number who can take part. Only the strong, healthy, and un-blemished youths are thought worthy to serve Ratu Pancering Jagat, and to receive him into their bodies.

For forty-two days prior to the ceremony the *taruna* leave their family households and go to live in the temple. From there they must go in a group to Desa Pinggan, a village on the other side of the lake, high in the mountains, where they gather special banana leaves for their costumes. For the entire six weeks they may not make any contact with any of the female members of the village group. They sleep each night in the temple at the feet of the statue, where an old priest teaches them ancient chanted Balinese prayers.

In the morning of the day of the performance the taruna are awakened early. They are led before the *pelinggih*, or shrine, of the Sun God, Batara Surya. There they are sprinkled with holy water and censed with sweet and pungent smoke while prayers are intoned; at this time they are almost naked, wearing only a small loincloth. When the taruna have been purified in this fashion they go into the underground shrine of the great statue once more, and there they put on the costumes for the coming event.

The sacred masks are also kept here in the shrine. The costumes consist of large aprons made from the dried banana leaves gathered in the forest. These have been stacked to dry beside the temple and subsequently sewn into the skirt-like aprons. Each dancer wears two of them—one hangs around his neck, while the other is tied around the waist. The lower skirt is given additional support from a pair of criss-crossed braces made from dried fibres of the same banana plant. Once the skirts have been tied on, the dancers murmur short prayers and put on their masks and head-dresses. Then, when they are ready, they go out one by one through the doorway of the shrine. Each takes up a nasty-looking fibre whip approximately ten feet long as he goes through the door. The taruna has become a *Berutuk*! He looks like an animated haystack on legs, with his mask frozen into a permanent expression of astonishment. Half of the masks are white or yellow in colour and are said to be female, while the

[4]

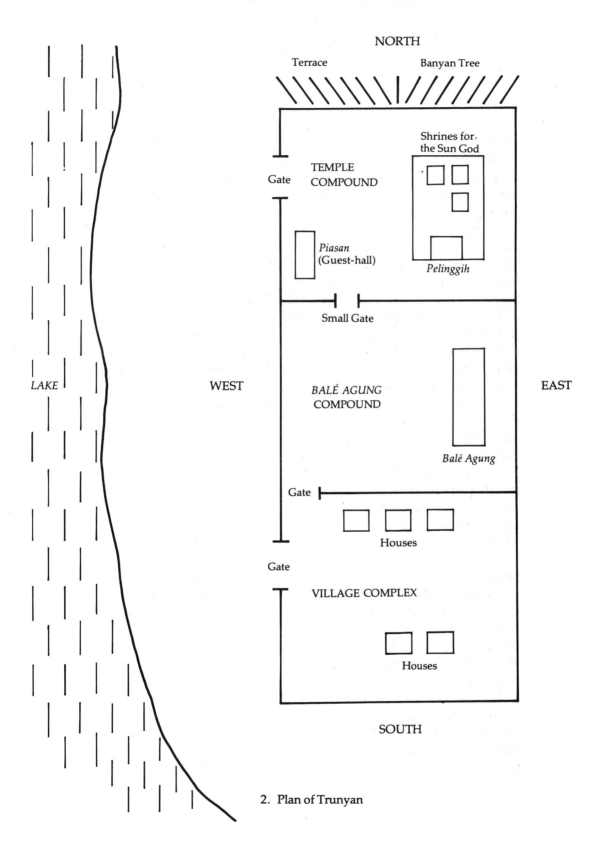

NORTH

Terrace   Banyan Tree

Shrines for
the Sun God

TEMPLE
COMPOUND

Gate

Piasan
(Guest-hall)

Pelinggih

Small Gate

BALÉ AGUNG
COMPOUND

LAKE   WEST

EAST

Balé Agung

Gate

Houses

Gate

VILLAGE COMPLEX

Houses

SOUTH

2. Plan of Trunyan

others, painted brown or red, represent males.

One by one the Berutuk come out from the underground temple, each flourishing his whip as he circles the shrine three times. Then, having finished the established 'choreography', each of the monsters wanders about at will in the courtyard, 'guarding' the shrine with fierce determination. His whip whistles menacingly and the spectators are warned not to come near. Finally, the four most sacred masks come out of the shrine . They form a kind of royal family: the *Patih* (Prime Minister), the Queen's brother, the Queen, and the King.

These characters have special head-dresses that are decorated with flowers, and distinctive masks; each also has an individualistic manner of walking. When the King and Queen appear, a priest comes forth with special offerings for them. The Berutuk as a group, and these masks in particular, have been entered by the god Ratu Pancering Jagat. The King and Queen also circle the shrine three times, and then they too rush about whipping excitedly as excitement mounts among the performers and in the audience.

The spectators cheer and shout, teasing the Berutuk and testing the boundaries of their territory. The more daring members of the audience, men and women, come forward and try to snatch pieces of the sacred banana leaves away from the costumes of the Berutuk; the monsters, in turn, attempt to prevent it, and a slashing cut of the whip is the punishment for a spectator who is caught. As further punishment anyone who has been whipped must later pay a fine to the village treasury. But the bits of banana leaf are highly charged with spiritual power—they offer protection against disease and encourage fertility in the rice-fields. Many men and women risk the strokes of the Berutuk's whip, hoping to bring home a lucky leaf to keep in the rafters of the house.

About noon this phase of the ritual concludes, and the dancers rest in anticipation of the violent exertions yet to come; their masks are raised, like the visors of knights' helmets, and they lie still under the shade of the temple roof while older members of the village fan their bodies. This pause is only a brief intermission, and soon thereafter the second section of the rite will begin. Once more the Berutuk take up a territory to defend, but now it is the nearby Balé Agung that they must protect, a secular space, also ringed by a wall, that is the centre of the village's social and governmental existence. Excitement rises to a peak immediately as dancers and spectators play the ancient cere-monial game, a game akin to a number of children's games played in the West. Many spectators attempt to snatch away pieces of the Berutuk's costumes, and in turn the performers are entitled to whip anyone entering the arena, except for the fes-tively-dressed women who enter at regular intervals with offer-ings to Ratu Pancering Jagat.

Later in the afternoon, some of the women present a special group of offerings to the Berutuk themselves, celebrating the fact that they have been entered by the God. These gifts consist of fruits, flowers and sweet cakes, and are taken by the shaggy dancers but not eaten. Members of the audience, edging cau-tiously near, offer to exchange cigarettes for bits of the offering, and the Berutuk, apparently tame for a brief while, allow them-selves to be approached; they exchange fruit and cakes for cigarettes. Some of the more enterprising members of the audi-ence use this opportunity to snatch a piece of the lucky banana leaf as well, and run out of the temple with their prize. The bits of offering are eaten on the spot by the members of the audience lucky enough to get some.

Later in the afternoon the final phase of the ritual performance takes place. Led by the priest, the women bring in new offer-ings, for the King and Queen Berutuk. No music accompanies their actions. When the offerings have been presented, the King and Queen dance together while the other Berutuk and the audience watch. The Patih and the Queen's brother continue to rush wildly about, trying to beat back the spectators and to prevent them from seeing the courtship dance of the King and Queen.

The couple, like two great haystacks, now dances an ancient step, which imitates the behaviour of the wild Wood-fowl. The King dances as the *keker*, or cock, the Queen is the *kiuh*, or

[7]

female. These beautiful birds are common in the vicinity of Trunyan. They bob and dip and peck and strut, scratching the ground and making sudden rushes past each other while flapping their 'wings'. This rough *pas de deux* has as much of the cock-fight about it as of the mating display. As it continues, excitement mounts among the noisy crowd of spectators. By now the dancers have moved down very close to the lake; the day approaches its end. The male Berutuk, in their red masks, take up their position in a line behind the King; the white-masked females line up opposite them, behind the Queen.

The courtship dance of the King and Queen continues for a half hour while the male and female Berutuk stand in their lines. Except for the courting pair, only the Patih and the Queen's brother are active; they flourish their whips at the crowd, but they are hardly able to maintain order. The spectators surge about, struggling to see the dancers while avoiding the whips. The mood is one of excitement and gaiety.

A line is drawn on the ground between two ceremonial banners to mark the separate territory of the King and the Queen, with the King occupying the space between the Queen and the waters of Lake Batur. The dancing takes on more of the quality of a contest than a performance as it progresses to a new phase. Now the Queen will try to evade the King, choosing a good moment to run from the safety of her own territory to the safety of the waters of the lake. The King will do his utmost to capture her, encouraged by the shouts of his followers. The two contestants eye each other across the boundary, and the Queen begins evasive action, with eye and body faking, feinted rushes, and other preliminary manoeuvres. The Queen tries to find a good opportunity to dodge past the King, seeking the safe 'goal' of the water.

At last the less agile youngster playing the Queen takes the plunge and makes a dash across the line marked by the banners. The Berutuk all shout as the King takes off after the Queen, and (usually) catches her by clasping his arms around her in a flying tackle. At that moment, the young men shout simultaneously and rush down to the water, hurling themselves in. There they strip off the remains of their banana-leaf costumes, swimming and frolicking after their exertions of the afternoon. The costumes are left floating on the water while the sacred masks are taken by the older tribesmen who come down to the lake's edge to assist. The young men are delighted to be rid of the very heavy costumes; they are hot and tired from their day of frenzied service to the God. The old men lay out the masks on pieces of sacred cloth spread on the sand; and when all of them have been assembled they are taken to the temple for a final offering and prayers. Then the masks are set aside until the next time the ceremony is performed. Six months before the next Berutuk festival, the old masks will be brought out again for cleaning and ceremonial repainting with powdered rice, betel nut, and ground turmeric. But now, at sunset of the day of the festival, they will be put away. Performers and audience go their separate ways for the evening meal after the activities have ended.

How are we to understand this strange and beautiful event? In the Berutuk performance there are aspects of a game, a ceremony, and a ritual drama, all in effect at the same time. Let us trace, very briefly, some of the sources of the elements we see.

There is a legend in Trunyan concerning the founding of the village, which can be retold in this manner. Once, long ago, a group of sixteen bachelors migrated West from the traditional Bali Aga territory in East Bali, in what is now the province of Karangasem. These taruna were farming people, and they went in search of new lands to farm. After a dangerous trek through hostile country they stopped at the high mountain slope above Lake Batur. Here they formed their settlement and established their plantations. They were faced with many dangers, living so deep in the wilderness. Often there were crop failures, and on occasion wild animals from the jungle carried off their livestock and even some of the villagers themselves. These Bali Aga people found relations with their neighbours to be difficult, for their neighbours had quite different beliefs and customs. To get wives the young men had to kidnap young women from other communities. Finally, only after a long struggle were the newcomers able to establish themselves in Trunyan.

[9]

This legend may correspond to historical fact, for it is clear that the villagers have many customs in common with Bali Aga groups in East Bali, and it is possible for the migration described to have occurred. It is a fact that the villagers of Trunyan, although they live beside a lake that is rich in fish, have no tradition of expertise on the water and get almost all their living from farming, just as the other people to the East do.

The legend finds expression in the Berutuk ceremony in a number of ways. The taruna become temporary vessels for the God, who appears in a demonic aspect. In the first stage of the performance day the masked figures and the audience carry out the game of whippings and thefts, thus re-enacting the struggle of the village founders to wrench blessings and fertility from a hostile and demon-filled wilderness. Here as in other wali dance forms the audience participates directly in the performance. In this case the audience is one of the contestants in a ritual battle; it is the protagonist in fact. For the event to be as successful as possible it is important that the Berutuk should not be too effective in protecting their *mana*-laden costumes.

The afternoon's activities are also based on the origin legend. The ritual kidnapping of the Queen represents the theft of brides by the sixteen original taruna of the village. It is in the interest of the village that the King should achieve his goal and capture the bride, and the 'casting' of the event is arranged accordingly. The successful capture of the Queen ensures fertility for the village through the re-enactment of its origin.

For the taruna and for the village group as a whole another process is in motion during the performance. For it is clear that the Berutuk event is also an initiation ceremony, a rite of passage. In Trunyan it is the custom for young men to marry late, and it has been the tradition for them to marry among other members of the village community. The matches made are of intense interest to the elders of the village, for they affect important considerations of inheritance, as well as traditional social and ceremonial responsibilities. The planning of the Berutuk ceremony gives the elders an important voice in when the young men of the group shall be deemed ready to marry. The very complex calculations involved in setting the proper day for the ceremony and the elaborate list of reasons for postponement become, in practice, a means by which the elders can exert control over when the youths can marry and when they may thus be admitted to full membership in the village. Many of the men who danced in 1976 had in fact been living as husbands with women for some time prior to the ceremony, but only after the ceremony had taken place were they eligible to formally marry and take their seats in the Village Council.

As a rite of passage, the Berutuk event has much in common with similar ceremonies from other cultures. The period of retreat, the quest for mana in the wilderness (getting the special banana leaves), tutelage in tribal traditions, and the prayers, are among these. As in similar ceremonies, the Berutuk rite involves an ordeal: in this case it is taking on for a day the role of the demonic aspect of Ratu Pancering Jagat. To take the role of the Berutuk is to take part in two ceremonies/dramas at the same time—one is the enactment of the origin legend, the other is the ordeal of the initiate who, following his impersonation, receives a kind of baptism in the purifying waters of the lake.

Still other overlays of significance are found in the ceremony, particularly in the odd identification of the King and Queen with the male and female wild Wood-fowl, the keker and kiuh. In another dance ceremony enacted in Trunyan, called *Mabuang*, the tribal elders form into two lines, each led by the oldest member of the subgroup. The leaders carry gold representations of keker and kiuh birds and dance with them, in a kind of stately imitation of the cock-fight. Here the keker and kiuh have an additional significance; in addition to the sexual symbolism of male and female, a social division of the tribe into rival subgroups is involved in the dance of these symbolic animals.[5] In the Berutuk event this element also appears, if in a truncated form, in the fighting dance of the King and Queen.

We have used the terms 'rite', 'event', 'ceremony', and 'performance' to describe the festival of the Berutuk and the activities connected with it in Trunyan. In truth it is all of these, and more. The Odalan of Ratu Pancering Jagat is at once a festival, a

[11]

religious service, an occasion for presentation of offerings and prayers, a sequence of games, and a dramatic performance. Everyone in the village has a role to fill in the proceedings, from the small child who dares the monster's whips to bring home a piece of good-luck for the household to the old men who take care of the masks. Each participates in the way appropriate to his or her age and station.

Sang Hyang Dedari

Another dance genre with ancient roots is the set of dances known as *Sang Hyang*, of which there are nearly two dozen varieties, most of them found only in remote northern and eastern mountain villages.[6] All of these dances involve putting one or more dancers into 'trance' to receive possessing divinities by means of incense, chanting and prayers. Then inhabited by gods or animal spirits, the performers interact with the audience and occasionally with each other, dancing, mimicking animal movements, and in some localities speaking as oracles. The performance invariably involves improvisation by the visiting spirits, which takes place along very definite pre-established lines. These possessions differ greatly from one another in kind and content, according to locality and the particular type of Sang Hyang. They range from celestial nymphs in *Sang Hyang Dedari* to the horse-spirits of *Sang Hyang Jaran*, the pig-spirits of *Sang Hyang Celeng*, and the serpent-spirits of *Sang Hyang Lelipi*. In all varieties of Sang Hyang there is an element of ritual purification, even of exorcism.

Sang Hyang Dedari is the best known of these dances of ritual possession, and it is the most easily seen by the visitor to Bali. The title means, roughly, 'Honoured Goddess Nymphs' and refers to the likeness of the young girl dancers to the *Widyadari*, who are demi-goddesses in Hindu mythology. Other traces of Hindu culture are difficult to find in the genre, which is pre-eminently a form of the village community, having little to do with the sophisticated culture of the palaces.

Like the Berutuk performers the dancers in Sang Hyang Dedari are selected from a special subgroup in the village; in this case it is from the pre-adolescent girls, between nine and twelve or thirteen years of age. Four or five of them are usually in service at a time, although no more than two of them dance in a single performance. The girls have special responsibilities and duties in the temple, often they are members of the family of a *pemangku*, or priest. In some localities it is traditional for the young dancers to choose their own successors from among the eligible girls, shortly before puberty enforces retirement. These youngsters are not trained dancers, although—like almost all Balinese villagers—they are quite familiar with the various kinds of dance-drama.

Sang Hyang Dedari dancers are by tradition a kind of temple servant, and have special restrictions on their conduct. The girls are expected to refrain from bad language and verbal abuse, and they are not allowed to incur certain forms of ritual profanation: for example, they must not walk under a clothes-line. They are required to sweep the temple and to help with cleaning the shrines; they also assist with preparing offerings and otherwise help the pemangku. They learn the old holy scriptural songs called *Kidung*.

Unlike most traditional Balinese dance performances, the Sang Hyang Dedari has no place in the great calendar of recurring festivals and ceremonies. It is performed at irregular intervals when needed on account of an epidemic or other disaster. If an outbreak of smallpox were to occur the dancers might perform nightly until the danger has been warded off and then might not perform again for years. The climate and topography of Bali have long made the island prey to the danger of epidemic disease; it is a theme of great antiquity in Balinese literature.

Traditionally the performance is given at night, and begins in the inner, most holy, courtyard (jeroan) of the village's principal temple (*Pura Puseh*). The entire village is in attendance. At the beginning of the ceremony, the audience sits quietly on the ground in the jeroan; near the pelinggih, or main shrine, the priest and his assistants, a chorus of women singers, and the group of dancers are placed, including both the pair who will perform that evening and the other members of the Sang Hyang group. The first part of the performance is called the *penudusan*, or smoking. During this period the goddesses are invited to descend, while the girls who will dance inhale quantities of pungent, drug-laden incense. They kneel side by side before the priest, who arranges the many offerings presented to the goddesses and controls the brazier in which the incense is burned on glowing coals of charcoal. The female choral group sings Kidung to establish an appropriate mood and to encourage the goddesses to appear. In the variant of this dance performed in Kintamani, Bangli district, small dolls made of wood are suspended before the girls and caused to dance and vibrate during the penudusan.

After half an hour or so, if the goddesses are pleased to descend, the Sang Hyang dancers fall back in a state that the Balinese call *kerawuhan*, or possessed. With their eyes closed they begin to sway sideways and backwards, helped and supported from behind by older women assisting in the ceremony. The priest wipes the girls' faces with a piece of cloth, for they perspire profusely. Once he is satisfied that the deities have arrived and entered the bodies of the young girls, he asks them to speak. In a high, tense voice utterly unlike normal speech, with a patterned nervous sing-song drawl, the goddesses address the villagers: 'Don't be afraid, my followers, we are arriving now! The cure for your sickness is at hand. Listen! Listen!' Then they prescribe medicine and ritual steps necessary to stem the epidemic. The prescription is usually for a mixture of herbs and rice, along with bark, grasses and other natural products of the island. The girls distribute special bracelets for the villagers to wear, made of thread on which a Chinese coin has been strung. Holy water is prepared by the priest.

Once the girls have gone into a trance, the women's chorus which has been singing Kidung becomes silent and, often at the request of the visiting goddesses, is replaced by a *Cak* chorus, which is a group of men drawn from the temple congregation, who chant and sing and make vocal percussive patterns of a very distinctive nature. Fires have been prepared close at hand in front of the girls, and at this time, to test and prove the depth of their trance, the girls jump onto the red-hot embers and tread on them with their bare feet. If they are sufficiently possessed their feet will not be burned and they will feel no pain. 'Come, come, my followers, why don't you join me to chase the bad spirits now? Hummmm?' The girls seem almost to plead as they begin to dance at last. The *gamelan legong*, a classical Balinese percussion orchestra, begins to play in the outer courtyard of the temple, where the girls will soon be carried.

The dance itself is an improvisation, done by the goddesses through the bodies of the youthful mediums. They are lifted to the shoulders of waiting men and carried about while still in a possessed state. To be a bearer of one of the goddesses is considered to be a great honour by the village taruna. The girls in their white skirts and head-dresses stand on the shoulders of their fast-moving carriers; they sway and undulate above the crowd which forms immediately into a kind of rough procession.

The movements made by the girls on their high and unsteady perches are based upon natural phenomena. For example, the movement known as *sayar soyor* imitates trees swaying in the wind; *ngelayak* is a bending movement of a tree bowing under the weight of many flowers; *capung mandus* is based on the flight of a dragon-fly; and the *kidang rebut muring* represents a deer pestered by biting flies. This vocabulary of movement is very old in Bali and has been taken up into more recent genres of the dance. In turn the villagers (whose movements formed the basis for the more sophisticated forms) have been influenced by the later types. Thus the dancing of the entranced Sang Hyang dancers shows definite signs of the *Legong* style.

Led by the pemangku, the carriers leave the jeroan, and the procession winds out into the street. The girls are carried to all corners of the village and to the central crossroad, making repelling gestures toward the demons who have caused the epidemic while the pemangku sprinkles holy water about, thus purifying the *desa* by means of the ritual. After an hour or two the small dancers are brought again to the temple, where the *gamelan* has continued to play.

[15]

In Cemengawon village, Gianyar Province, at this point in the ceremony the girls are returned to the ground. There they dance together in close co-ordination with the gamelan; this has not been possible during their travels to the four corners of the village. Imitation of Legong style is clearly seen. Elsewhere the girls are taken back into the temple at once. There they are brought out of their trance with the aid of holy water, prayers, and the presentation of offerings to the departing goddesses. These are presented by the pemangku, accompanied by the chorus of female singers, who render an appropriate Kidung. The girls return to their normal consciousness slowly, tired from their exertions but otherwise unharmed by their experience as dwelling-places for the powerful energies of the goddesses who temporarily inhabited them. Many of the young dancers seem to enjoy their experience as performers and go on to become professional dancers after retiring from service in the temple.

The subject of trance and ritual possession has been of great interest to many visitors to Bali, although little of a precise or scientific nature is known about the physiological aspects of the phenomenon. In fact it might be difficult to improve our understanding of kerawuhan, for the condition involves both an individual and a context, and one could hardly perform scientific measurements in the normal situation where possession occurs without disrupting the context. Many observers have commented on the similarity of the kerawuhan state to advanced levels of hypnosis. For the Sang Hyang dancer the crucial test is the walking on fire, which proves to the pemangku and the spectators that the possession has in fact taken place. The condition manifested by the little girls is much more refined and controlled than the frenzied self-stabbing of the kris dancers found in various other performance situations in Bali.

It is important to emphasize that all Balinese dance is not performed in a state of 'trance'; quite another term and conception apply to the trained performer's inspiration, which is often called *taksu*. The dances of possession are of a different nature from the more secular performances and make different demands on the performer. For the former the essential pre-

[16]

requisite is that the performer be able to *nadi*, or become possessed; dancing ability is a secondary matter. For the professional, these factors are reversed. These conditions can however become confusingly mixed in some Balinese performing situations, for example, where possession rituals have become embedded in performances for tourists. Here the 'trance' behaviour seen by the spectator may quite simply be an example of 'highly realistic' acting.

What trance provides to the Sang Hyang dancers is pre-eminently a very specific characterization with a distinctive vocal pattern and a conventionalized set of improvisational choices. In Sang Hyang Dedari, these consist of the types of prescriptions for magical remedies to be suggested and other forms of aid to the village. In all the Sang Hyang dances the gods are in a sense the servants of the village, called to perform an unvarying action, which is to drive off the dangerous *buta* (demons) responsible for the epidemic. It is a simple but very powerful rudimentary dance-drama having no literary content whatever. As in other dances of this group, complex plots and pre-established dialogue are absent.

In the other varieties of Sang Hyang, most often a lower, usually animal-like, spirit is brought into the body of the dancer. In Sang Hyang Jaran, for example, which is still represented in some wards of the capital city of Denpasar, horse-spirits invest the adult male dancers, who in the kerawuhan state run neighing through the embers of bonfires while barefoot, astride straw hobby-horses. In these cases the exorcism of the buta is accomplished when the possessed dancers *frighten* the demons away. In Sang Hyang Celeng the dancer is entered by a pig-spirit who impels the performer to *eat* (for the most part only symbolically) the accumulated filth and impurities responsible for the epidemic, volcanic eruption, or other disaster.

Rejang

In the Berutuk ceremony and in the Sang Hyang dances we have seen some of the many varieties of Balinese dance in which

[17]

deities or spirits enter the dancer(s), inhabiting them and controlling their behaviour. In another important category of Balinese religious dancing, the performance is given *for* the gods rather than by them.

At every Balinese temple festival visiting gods descend into doll-like special wooden effigies called *pratima*, which are gaily dressed, decorated with flowers and placed in special portable shrines for the festive occasion.[7] The gods who dwell thus for a time in the pratima are carried in procession and bathed. They are presented with offerings of food, flowers and other tangibles, and also—very often—with offerings in the form of performances. The dancers perform to delight and amuse their celestial guests and to greet them with appropriate respect.

Rejang is one of the most ancient and most formal of these entertainments. It can still be seen in many villages throughout Bali, and most villages have a group devoted to it. Although it is one of the simplest Balinese dances, Rejang possesses a dignity and elegance that are very beautiful. In feeling it could not be farther removed from the struggling tumult of the lashing Berutuk or the frenzied crowd that surges around the Sang Hyang Dedari and their bearers.

Rejang is a processional group dance performed by the female members of the temple congregation. Women of all ages take part in the performance in most villages, but in the old-fashioned Bali Aga villages of Tenganan and Asak the performers are drawn only from the children and young women of the village. Rejang is never performed professionally. In the typical performance some forty to sixty women take part. All are dressed in formal traditional Balinese costume, with a long sash (*anteng*) tied around the waist, and an elaborate semi-circular head-dress, consisting of a frame made of gold to which fresh flowers are attached.

Rejang is performed in the daytime, usually in the early afternoon. Through a single gateway the long lines of dancers enter the jeroan in pairs from the less sacred precincts outside. Upon entering they execute a simple choreography that divides them into four lines facing the pelinggih where the pratima have been placed. The front dancers from each line approach the gods, dancing, in a single row of four. They progress slowly, waving their fans and holding the anteng out from the body at waist-height. They undulate as they advance; their faces are drawn into serious, rather preoccupied, smiles. When they reach the pelinggih the line divides, with two of the dancers going off to each side. The next row comes up just behind it, and the dance continues as each row in turn comes forward, to the accompaniment of appropriate music. The *gamelan gong gedé* is traditionally played in Batur, Bangli Province, while the sacred *selonding* ensemble accompanies the dancers in Tenganan. When each row of dancers has been presented in turn to the pelinggih the performance is over, and dancers and audience move on to the next event in the day's schedule of activities.

In Batuan village, Gianyar Province, Rejang is better known by the name *Sutri*. The movements in this variant form are especially slow and highly refined, which befits a performance in this famous village, with its many *brahmana* (priestly-caste) families, and its long tradition of excellence and conservatism in the dance and drama. Sutri is also unique among the varieties of Rejang because of its exorcist qualities. The annual performance at the *Usaba Nini* Festival at the *Pura Desa*, Batuan, is thought to help protect against the danger of epidemic diseases. If any sickness does break out in the village during the year, special performances of Sutri are given in the jeroan of that temple every five days until the danger is past.

Baris Gedé

Complementary to the Rejang is the *Baris Gedé*, a group dance performed by the adult males of a village on the occasion of Odalan. Baris Gedé is often given just before or just after a performance of Rejang in the afternoon, although the two forms are not invariably associated. Just as the special semi-circular floral head-dresses are distinctive of Rejang, the Baris Gedé is revealed by certain helmets of characteristic triangular shape worn by the dancers, which consist of many pointed fragments of mother-of-pearl thrusting upwards in a pyramid: they are attached to springs which cause them to shake constantly as the dancers move.

The dancers in Baris Gedé can be considered the bodyguard of the visiting deities who are temporarily residing in the pratima. The men carry sacred heirloom weapons, such as spears, lances, shields, daggers or even, in some villages, rifles. Each dancer-soldier carries the same kind of weapon, and the type of Baris is distinguished by the type of weapon employed. The size of the group can vary from eight men to several dozen, depending on the custom of the village and the number and kind of weapons available in the village collection of inherited treasures. The largest and most grand of the varieties is *Baris Tumbak* which is performed at Batur, Bangli district; here the group is often made up of more than sixty dancers.

In the performance at Batur, the dancers enter through a large and ornate single gateway that opens into the jeroan from the south. Each dancer wears the characteristic helmet and carries a ten-foot lance. The rest of his costume consists of rather tight-fitting white trousers, white shirt, and a decorative uniform apron that hangs down from the shoulders in front and behind; the costume is completed by the dancer's kris, or dagger.

The dancers march in, one after the other, in close unison. As they walk they shout in rhythm. Their movement is accompanied by the great old gamelan gong gedé that is the pride of Batur village. The group forms into rank and file as the dancers enter, with the first dancers continuing to march in place until everyone has entered and the formation is complete. Then, at a signal in the music, all shout together and then kneel to pray; the music stops. Facing the pelinggih, with weapon held straight, the dancers remain silently in the kneeling position to offer themselves and their weapons to the service of the gods in the pratima. They kneel for five minutes or more. Then the gamelan gong gedé begins to play again, providing spirited martial accompaniment for the next portion of the dance.

At this signal the men rise and execute a rather complex choreographic manoeuvre dividing the group into two subgroups facing each other. Shouting again, the two 'armies' execute a stylized mock-combat and battle drill. The soldiers of each side move in unison, attacking and then in turn defending against the attack of the opposing side. The emphasis is on co-ordinated group action rather than on individual combat— there is no leeway for individual variation in the contest of one soldier against another. The dancers pause on signal and march to a new alignment before they commence another round of stylized fighting. When this has concluded, all face the pelinggih again and bow. The dancers stop in place where they are as the piece concludes.

In the mountain villages of northern Bali the performance of Baris Gedé usually involves a series of similar dances following upon each other in succession. In each phase a new group of weapons is presented and manipulated. In Batur, for example, a smaller group of dancers from the Baris Tumbak group leaves immediately at the conclusion of that dance to go out and equip themselves with the boat-shaped shields of *Baris Dadap*, which follows quite soon after. The choreography is very similar to that of Baris Tumbak, although the number of dancers is much smaller.

Baris Dadap is of particular interest, for in addition to its place in the Odalan it is often seen in connection with cremation ceremonies. The special wedge-like painted shields carried by the dancers are made from the wood of the *dadap* tree, which is valued for its medicinal and magical qualities. The shields of Baris Dadap are less weapons than somewhat abstract representations of boats, and are vestigial survivals from ancient Balinese funerary practices; similarly-shaped votive objects are employed in burial rites elsewhere in Indonesia.[8]

The dadap tree itself has special meaning and importance in Balinese ceremony and performing arts. The ritual shadow-puppet play, performed in the daytime (*Wayang Lemah*), is performed against a thick string stretched between the trunks of two small dadap trees. Dadap leaves are an ingredient in many folk medicinal remedies. The head-dresses of the classical *Gambuh* dance are traditionally decorated with fresh dadap

[21]

leaves. The significance of the plant, apart from its inherent pharmacological properties, has to do with its association with the high end of the kaja-kelod axis. The dadap grows in the mountains and especially on the slopes of Gunung Agung where the gods dwell. It is so important in Balinese religious usage that many households in southern Bali have patches of the dadap in their gardens.

The movement and structure of *Baris Tamiang* which concludes the series of Baris Gedé dances at Batur is similar; this form takes its name from the round shields that the dancers present and brandish.

Baris dances have been known in Indonesia at least since the sixteenth century. An old poetic historical romance, the *Kidung Sunda*, which is dated about 1550, mentions that seven kinds of *bebarisan* were performed on the occasion of the funeral of an important personage.[9] The word 'baris' means 'line' or 'row' and refers to the military formations assumed by the dancers. *'Gedé'* simply means 'great', and designates Baris dances performed by groups of men. There are other, non-ceremonial, forms of Baris dancing: *Baris Melampahan*, or dramatic Baris, in which a story is told, employing a company of dancers clad in the Baris costumes; and solo Baris, a dance by a single male performer, often quite young, dressed in Baris costume, who presents a plotless character-study of a young warrior.

Procession

Following the performance of Rejang and/or Baris Gedé at a typical Balinese Odalan, the pratima are taken to the sacred bathing place a mile or so away from the temple to receive their ritual cleansing. The entire temple congregation takes the opportunity to join in the procession. All members of the celebrating group, male and female, are dressed in their best ceremonial attire; the dancers still wear their Baris and Rejang costumes. Individual pots and kettles, small gongs, drums and cymbals are taken up from the gamelan and beaten by the musicians in a lilting pattern (*bebonangan*) as the procession winds down the highway and then along a narrow path down to the bathing place. Accompanied by colourful offerings, the gods in their gaily-decorated shrines are shaded by parasols and guarded by the weapons consecrated in the Baris Gedé performance as they are carried along. Once again, as is seen so often in Bali, the movement of the group is along the axis from kaja to kelod, as the line of people winds down from the pelinggih in the jeroan to the chthonic watering-place. The route is chosen so as to ensure a maximum display of the visiting deities and their magnificently turned-out followers.

After the pratima have received their ritual bathing and the offerings brought for the purpose have been presented, the procession forms again and the congregation returns to the temple. The gods are returned to their place in the pelinggih. Now the main body of offerings that has been prepared for presentation on behalf of the entire village is dedicated by the attendant priests. This process requires several hours, and often while it is taking place the dancers in the Rejang and Baris Gedé groups go home for refreshment and a change of clothing.

The dedicatory prayers offered by the priests are accompanied by elegant hand-gestures of great antiquity and delicate formality, especially when the officiant is a *pedanda* (high-caste priest)—his prayers are in Sanskrit and his *mudra*, or ritual gestures, descend from those of the Indian Hindu and Buddhist sages of a millennium or more ago.[10] The pedanda sits high on a platform, praying and ringing his bell and making his mudra. Beneath him, on the ground, at his right are set up the dadap poles and thread of the Wayang Lemah, while on the left a gamelan gong is situated in position to accompany the ritual *Topeng Pajegan*.

Prayer, performance, and offering are interwoven in Balinese Hinduism, and in Balinese art as in Balinese religion there is a linking of three elements in every considered expressive assertion. These are *bayu, sabda, idep*: action, word, and thought. Thus when the brahmana priest prays there is a thought in his mind, a word on his lips and an action with his hands (the mudra), all at the same time. Similarly, when an offering is presented, the *idea* symbolized in the object employed must be completed by the *act* of presentation and the *word* of the appropriate prayers. The bayu/sabda/idep trinity also expresses itself in the dance, both in specific technicalities of linking a phrase-of-movement or sequence-of-gestures to the spoken or sung dialogue, and in the larger dimension that leads the Balinese to prefer dance-drama to more abstract forms of the art.

Gabor, Memendet, and Baris Pendet

The simple three-part Balinese prayer finds elaboration in a group of temple dances that are usually performed in the evening of an Odalan. These dances elaborate and develop the action (bayu) involved in the presentation of prayers and offerings. In these dances the performers carry the offerings to be consecrated and dance with them before the deities in their shrines. The verbal dimension (sabda) is provided by a chorus of women, who sing the sacred Kidung 'Wargasari', describing the arrival of the goddess and her entertainment. The female chorus consists of a dozen or so singers who have rehearsed regularly for the occasion. In keeping with the multi-media nature of the Balinese performance, a gamelan plays instrumental music for the accompaniment of the dancers, while the *a capella* choir of Kidung singers carries on relentlessly in their own corner, without relation to the other elements of the performance.

In Gabor the elaborate presentation of offerings is done by female dancers, who are usually members of the Rejang group. In Singapadu village, Gianyar district, the Gabor performance begins late in the evening. When the priest has presented the large group of offerings on behalf of the village as a whole, the members of the Rejang society gather near the pelinggih. They are no longer wearing their Rejang costumes, but have changed into normal temple dress. The women are called together by a lower-caste female priest who encourages them to begin the Gabor. Only the best dancers will actually take part. The girls are shy at first and must be urged to begin, but after a time the first pair is ready to dance.

The gamelan gong strikes up the Gabor melody, and the dancers begin, two by two. Each carries a bowl of flowers or other offering in her right hand. They dance side by side, facing the pelinggih and advancing toward it, always facing the gods in their pratima. The vocabulary of movement employed is far more complicated than any that we have discussed so far; Gabor requires talent and training in Balinese dance technique. The basic walk is a stylized elaboration of the walking step of Rejang, but the dancers execute a variety of complex patterns of movement, in close co-ordination with the drummer and accompanying gamelan. The vocabulary of movement is drawn from the full range of classical Balinese dancing. Each pair of dancers performs for five minutes or so in front of the pelinggih before the offerings are deposited at its foot. Four to eight pairs dance on a particular occasion, and a performance can last up to an hour altogether.

Complementary to Gabor is *Memendet*, which is performed by adult men from the temple congregation or occasionally by the pemangku. The dancers wear their regular temple costume, but are without shirts. They dance a rather simple step based on the Baris Gedé group of movements, and the music is also from the Baris repertoire. In some villages, a dance called *Baris Pendet* is given, which is like a Baris Gedé performed by eight men. They dance with ritual vessels filled with flowers instead of with weapons. Baris Pendet, which can be seen at temple festivals in Sebatu village, Gianyar Province, or in Tejakula village, Buleleng Province, is usually performed in the daytime, rather than late at night. These dances, like Gabor, are performed by dancers who appear in pairs with their offerings, dancing their way to the pelinggih, where the offerings are left. The dances in which offerings are presented may be seen as extension and development of the idea inherent in the use of the mudra to accompany prayer. They elaborate the *act* of presentation; the performance process itself takes on the character of offering.

When Gabor or Memendet dancers have finished presenting

the offerings, the pemangku and assistants go to the altar while the congregation prepare to offer individual and family prayers. Men sit and women kneel on the ground in the jeroan, facing the pelinggih. The priests distribute liquor—arak or rice wine— which is poured out onto the ground to cleanse away the buta. Then each individual, alone or with the family group, lights a stick of incense and puts it in the ground nearby. The priests distribute consecrated flower-petals which are taken up in the hands and held fervently to their foreheads by the worshippers. At each phase of the nine-part prayer, petals are thrown forward toward the pelinggih in a gesture of humility and respect, as each villager unites bayu/sabda/idep in the process of praying. And with these prayers the formal activities of a typical Odalan come to an end.

In this chapter a number of sacred ritual dances of the inner temple courtyard have been discussed, which are grouped by Balinese authorities in the wali category. As such their performance is considered to be essentially an act of worship; and they are not to be performed for financial gain. They are done as a sign of devotion and are considered to be service to the temple. While non-members of the temple congregation are usually welcome to watch the temple dances at an Odalan or other religious ceremony, it is important that due respect be paid to local customs and rules.

In all of the dances of the wali group the actual participation of the deities is essential. Even in Rejang, where the gods remain passive in the pelinggih, they must in some sense accept the offerings extended by the young women. In wali dances the attention of the gods is kept under control by the participating priests, and their time is tightly scheduled and programmed.

1. The classification of Balinese dances into wali (sacred), bebali (ceremonial), and bali-balihan (secular) genres was first proposed by the late I Gusti Bagus Sugriwa, at a seminar held in Denpasar, 1971, *Proyek Pemeliharaan* (1971), p. 3.

2. Soekmono (1973) provides a convenient summary of Indonesian cultural history. See also Hanna (1976) for Bali. Covarrubias (1937, reprinted 1973) is still the best introduction to Balinese culture generally. de Zoete and Spies (1938, reprinted 1973) has been the standard reference on Balinese dance and theatre, except for the shadow-play, since it appeared forty years ago; now somewhat out-of-date, the book is still a trove of information and vivid description.

3. Stutterheim (1935), pp. 1—5.

4. Bernet-Kempers (1978), pp. 174—6, describes the temple and statue from an archaeological point of view.

5. Scholars may wish to consider these dances in the light of the fascinating, if erratic, essay 'On the Meaning of Javanese Drama', Rassers (1959), pp. 1—62.

6. Belo (1960) investigated trance performances of many types in the years before the Second World War. Most of the performances she studied were given especially for visitors, outside the usual ritual context.

7. Belo (1953) describes the Odalan.

8. Especially among the Toraja people of Sulawesi (Celebes).

9. Relevant passages are quoted in Holt (1967), p. 288.

10. De Kleen (1923) provides excellent drawings of the priest's mudra; unfortunately, her written text is not reliable.

2 *Gambuh*, a Classical Dance of the Second Courtyard

ANOTHER important category of Balinese dances is the group of ceremonial performances called *bebali*. These genres are also performed in connection with Odalan and other important religious occasions, but they are of a different, somewhat lower, level of sanctity from the wali group discussed above. The bebali dances are all *dramatic* dances with a narrative element and may be understood as optional entertainment for the gods who are attending a festival. Unlike the wali dances, those of the bebali type do not compel the gods' attention; nor are any necessary parts of the ritual embedded in the performance. The bebali dances are nonetheless explicitly religious in intention for they are meant to entertain the divinities present as well as the human spectators. The celestial guests are treated as visiting dignitaries who must be kept amused during the long hours of the festival day.

In the pages above wali dances have been characterized as belonging to a native Balinese tradition centred in the village community. The bebali genres, on the other hand, are associated with another, almost antithetical, strand in the composition of Balinese culture, which might be called the Hindu-Javanese. This is a tradition of foreign rather than native origin coming directly from Java and indirectly from India. With it are associated the caste system, centralized state government under a powerful single nóble ruler, and a Javanized form of the Hindu religion.[1]

Hindu-Javanese culture came to Bali in successive waves of Javanese power and influence between the ninth and sixteenth centuries A.D. At times during this period of 700 years connections between the two islands were quite close; at other times Bali was left free from strong outside influences. After the expedition of the Javanese War Minister Gajah Mada in the mid-fourteenth century, in which that legendary hero put down a local Balinese despot, Bali became part of the Majapahit Empire which held sway over Java and Bali for more than 150 years. During that time, the cultural life of the palaces of both islands was united. Then, about 1520, Majapahit fell before the advance of Islam in Java.[2] The last courtiers moved to Bali, where the

Hindu-Balinese culture was left to develop for several hundred years in virtual isolation.[3] The bebali dances in existence today are forms which have descended from the dance-dramas of the courts of the Majapahit period and of the Hindu-Balinese courts which were formed in their likeness over the next two centuries.

Historical and literary records surviving from the Majapahit period tell us something of the dance performances given in the palaces and great houses of the era. The performing arts of the time were already highly developed, and were heir to a very old tradition extending back five centuries or more in Indonesia and beyond that to India. We read in old tales set in the palaces of the medieval East Javanese kingdoms of dance-dramas given by masked and by unmasked dancers; descriptions of such performances are also included in historical documents like the *Kidung Sunda*, and the *Nagara Kretagama*. Balinese documents also include accounts of similar court performances of a somewhat later period.[4]

In the old accounts we find descriptions of a courtly dance tradition of great sophistication, elegance, and refinement. The Hindu Princes and their wives were enthusiastic patrons of the arts. Some of them were amateur performers as well and took part themselves in public performances of the dance. The Princes subsidized and employed a professional corps of highly skilled artists and teachers who were attached to the court. Performances described in the old romances indicate that courtly audiences of the day were especially appreciative of comic talent, wit, skill in improvisation, grace, refinement, and subtlety. Ritual aspects of the performance were taken for granted by the old authors and are not emphasized in the accounts, although provisions for offerings given in connection with the performance are described.

Gambuh

One of the types of courtly dance-drama mentioned in the old records still exists in Bali today, preserved by a continuous performing tradition that extends back for 400 years. This is

Gambuh, a bebali dance of the second temple courtyard, which is performed without masks.[5] In Gambuh aspects of the manners and ideals of the sophisticated courtiers of the Majapahit era are preserved, as well as music, choreographic ideas, and highly refined literature of the period. Archaic, formal, and very stately, Gambuh is accompanied by a unique music dominated by wailing flutes and is presented by grave dancer-actors who chant and intone their lengthy speeches.

Admirable for its own unique beauty, Gambuh is also of great importance in Balinese dance because of its influence on later forms; it is the source and prototype for the more modern dramatic-dance genres like Topeng, Wayang Wong, Arja, Legong, and Baris Melampahan. Balinese choreographers have relied very much on Gambuh for notions of structure, characterization, means of dramatization, compositional elements, and many other features. In addition, Gambuh is the point of origin for much of the modern Balinese musical repertoire, and especially for the drumming patterns which are the essential point of contact and communication between the dancer and the accompanying gamelan.

The traditional locus for the Gambuh performance is the second courtyard of the temple, called *jaba tengah*. This space, like the jeroan adjacent to it, is enclosed by a wall about 6 feet high; tall ceremonial gateways (*candi bentar*) give access to the outer courtyard and to the jeroan, as do simple doors which serve for mundane entrances and exits to and from the area. As the middle space in the traditional Balinese temple, the jaba tengah is in effect a transitional zone between sacred and secular spaces. It serves as the ante-room to the jeroan. The jaba tengah is empty for most of the year. It contains small buildings and pavilions in which kitchen equipment, ceremonial paraphernalia, musical instruments, and similar articles are stored between festivals.

Only when serious preparations for an upcoming festival are under way does the jaba tengah come to life. By the time of the Odalan it is bustling with devout activity and with people hurrying through on their way to perform various duties.

[30]

Groups gather in the jaba tengah before proceeding into the jeroan to present their offerings. Food is chopped and cooked in the area, and later it will be eaten here.

The area also serves as an important performing space during a festival and in the days leading up to it. Then there are many centres of interest in the crowded courtyard and often several gamelan groups play at the same time in connection with subsidiary rituals. One such central focal point is the special space where dramatic dance performances are given. This area, called the *kalangan*, is the basic and essential Balinese dance stage. It can be set up in many places, profane or sacred.

As we have remarked above, the jaba tengah area where the kalangan is set up for a Gambuh performance is not ritually consecrated space. Therefore, here in the jaba tengah as well as any place *outside* the temple where a stage might be set up, the performance area must be set apart and consecrated before the performance can begin. A pemangku is required for the ritual consecration, which involves presenting offerings to the earth-spirits (buta), along with poured libations and burning incense, accompanied by appropriate prayers. The buta are invoked and placated here, for the performance will take place on the ground, which is buta territory. The dancers do not wish to step on them or otherwise cause offence.

Another set of offerings must be presented before the Gambuh performance can begin. These are given to the high god, Wisnumurti, Patron of Dance. The occasion is the bringing out of the sacred head-dresses, or *gelung*, just before the performance. Here the offering consists of fruits, flowers, a coconut, along with Chinese coins, rice-cakes, an egg, and a length of thread symbolically to tie the whole together. These head-dresses ceremonially represent the entire dance costume; they are specially consecrated when first put into service, and are handed down from generation to generation as venerated objects.

Another small ceremony is required after the gelung have been blessed. Now it is the turn for the dancers themselves to receive a purifying sprinkle of holy water, as additional offer-

[31]

ings are presented at the *sanggah taksu*, a shrine dedicated to what we might call 'the divine force of inspiration'. The dancers pray for assistance from the gods in performing their roles, and ask that the audience might enjoy their work. Thus even for a semi-secular bebali performance, a full complement of ritual preparations is required.

The kalangan itself consists of a rectangular stage-area roughly 30 feet deep by 18 feet wide. It is marked off from the surrounding space by a foot-high bamboo fence which indicates the boundary of the performance area. A decorative ceiling made of greenery is often affixed overhead. Decorative lances are placed at the sides of the stage, as are bright umbrellas, which are emblems of power and status. These lances and umbrellas serve as points of reference for the dancers during the performance. The gamelan orchestra is placed at one end of the kalangan, to the side. Near it is a row of mats, where performers who are waiting between appearances may rest and take refreshments. The entrance is located at the top of the flight of stairs leading up to the archway going into the jeroan.

The kalangan is a temporary stage, prepared anew for each performance. Like the temple in which it is housed, the kalangan is aligned carefully on the axis of the ritually significant directions kaja and kelod and is adorned with flowers and other temporary decoration. Lighting is provided by the sun, for Gambuh is traditionally a daytime performance.

In its subject matter as well as in its origins, Gambuh is associated with the life of the medieval Hindu-Indonesian courts. The stories are usually taken from a long romantic poem called *Malat*, which is made up of a set of tales concerning the adventures of handsome Prince Panji Inu Kertapati and his destined bride, Princess Candra Kirana. The language spoken by the principal characters in the drama is the language of the old poem itself, called Kawi by the Balinese, who consider it to be their own ancestral language.

'Kawi' is another name for the Old Javanese language, which was employed in the courts of Bali and Java during the medieval period. It is the essential language of the Balinese theatre; the

[32]

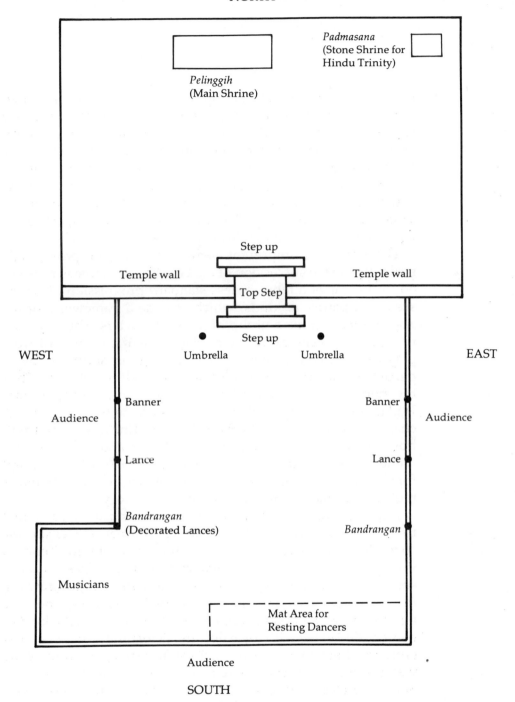

NORTH

Pelinggih
(Main Shrine)

Padmasana
(Stone Shrine for
Hindu Trinity)

Step up

Temple wall   Temple wall

Top Step

Step up

WEST   EAST

Umbrella   Umbrella

Banner   Banner

Audience   Audience

Lance   Lance

Bandrangan
(Decorated Lances)   *Bandrangan*

Musicians

Mat Area for
Resting Dancers

Audience

SOUTH

3. Kalangan, the Traditional Arena Stage

[33]

principal characters always speak in Kawi in the shadow-theatre and in the dance-drama. Translations are provided on a running basis by attendants and comic retainers as the performance goes along, for few in the audience can understand the ceremonial tongue. But, just as Latin was considered by many to be the appropriate language for the Mass long after most in the congregation had lost all comprehension of what was being said, Kawi is kept in the Balinese theatre out of respect for its long tradition and venerable (*wayah*) majesty.

The story is an important element in Gambuh, providing a structure for the succession of dances. The narrative is presented by means of a more-or-less standard progression of 'stock' scenes of particular kinds, which provide a framework for the appearance of a fixed group of 'type' characters. The types are identified in general by their titles, which are standard from play to play; each principal character may in addition have a particular character name, specific to the individual story. Thus the hero, Prince Panji, might be called Prince Panji Damar Wulan in one story, but Panji Mahisa Jayanti in another. A character such as the Old Patih (Prime Minister), would not, however, change his name from one tale to another. The stock scenes are hardly differentiated at all from play to play, except for minor differences in the dialogue. Only minor alterations are required to change a scene to fit a different story.

The Putri, or principal female character, is usually presented in the first scene of a typical Gambuh performance. Her specific character name is usually Putri Candra Kirana or Putri Kencana Wungu. She is a female character of the refined (*alus*)—sometimes called 'sweet' (*manis*)—type, with a high, drawling falsetto voice, small (preferably almond-shaped) eyes, a delicate figure, and restrained movements. She wears a specific kind of gelung, decorated with fresh flowers. Before the Putri makes her entrance, her ladies-in-waiting must first appear to prepare the way for her. The first of these is the Condong, or maidservant. She is the attendant of the Putri, but although she is a retainer, she is of noble family and ranks first among the court ladies. (In the past it was the custom for the Condong and for all the female

[34]

roles in the Gambuh to be danced and acted by men, but now-adays women take part very often, even to the extent of playing the refined male characters.)

The performance begins with an instrumental overture by the accompanying *gamelan gambuh*. The ensemble and the genre it accompanies take their name from the quartet of *gambuh suling*, long flutes which are the core of the melodic section of the orchestra. These are blown with a difficult circular breathing technique that produces a continuous sound. Another melody instrument, a bowed, fiddle-like, spiked-lute called the *rebab*, plays along in unison with the gambuh suling. The musical ensemble is completed by a lead singer (*juru tandak*) and an extensive percussion section, including drums, cymbals, bells, and gongs of various sizes and types.

At the conclusion of the overture, the Condong appears at the head of the entrance steps, facing from the direction kaja toward kelod. Something of the divine is being presented to the secular beings at the kelod end of the stage. The Condong sings and dances to her own identifying melody as she descends into the kalangan. She dances in a complicated, energetic pattern that covers a great deal of the stage area. Her movements are in the realm of pure dance, without pantomimic or other narrative features. They are drawn from an old indigenous vocabulary of movement seen in simpler form in the old wali and Joged dances. The choreographic sophistication and the complex patterns of accent, in which the dancer works in tight co-ordination with the orchestra, are from the later tradition of the Hindu courts.

The Condong dances for fifteen minutes or so before she summons the second group of preliminary dancers, the *kakan-kakan*, who are ladies-in-waiting. These dancers enter in a group and dance together, in a style that is somewhat more refined than that of the Condong. Movements reminiscent of Rejang are clearly in evidence in this well-crafted ensemble section, which displays marks of a trained choreographic imagination at work on materials in the form of elements in the vocabulary of movement provided by the Balinese folk culture.

As the four kakan-kakan execute their slowly unfolding sequence of symmetrical patterns, moving languidly and with a great sense of flow, the dancers call to one another with high, refined, cries: 'Quickly, quickly, sister, don't be late!' The Condong takes a position to one side, where she delivers comments on the progress of her sisters: 'How beautifully you dance, sisters, how lovely are your costumes!' Then the music speeds up to mark the beginning of a new section of the dance, more energetic in quality. The Condong joins in and the five women dance together in preparation for the entrance of the Putri. At last, perhaps three-quarters of an hour into the performance, the Condong brings the gamelan to a halt with a sharp clap of her hands.

The kakan-kakan then proceed to sit on the row of fibre mats laid on the ground at the far end of the kalangan. Here they may drop out of character and eat, drink, and chew betel-nut while awaiting their next appearance in the performance. The Condong, meanwhile, approaches the foot of the steps, calling to her mistress to come out. The flutes strike up a new melody for the heroine, who appears at the head of the steps. The Condong kneels respectfully. Slowly the Putri dances down the stairs, while singing a verse from the Malat. Between phrases of singing she calls to the Condong: 'Be prepared to follow me!' When the Putri reaches the ground, the Condong rises and the two dancers execute a duet, in which each counters the other's movement. Here also the idiom is pure dance. The dancers sweep over the entire stage area.

The Putri wears a long train that sweeps the ground between her feet, and her dancing emphasizes the characteristic Balinese jerking and winding head movements. The Condong dances while maintaining proper subservience and respect. Her arms are crossed and she favours a low position in relation to her partner. Her jumps in squatting position are developed from the old native Balinese movement called *gelatik nuwut papah*, an animal-imitation based on the paddy-bird jumping sideways on a tree branch. At the end of the duet, approximately an hour after the performance has begun, there is a short pause. The preliminaries are complete. The Putri is left standing alone in the centre of the kalangan, as the musicians play an intermezzo.

The next section of the performance is given over to dialogue. The Condong calls the kakan-kakan, who rise from the mats and approach the Princess, kneeling before her. The dialogue begins, with the Princess addressing the ladies, who speak always in a unison chorus. The talk is highly stereotyped and is conducted in Kawi but it is translated for the benefit of the audience by the Condong.

After elaborate courtesies have been extended the subject turns to the basic plot situation, which is not developed at length in this scene. The heroine usually expresses remorse, in very general terms, because she is separated from her beloved Panji. Very often she is in captivity in the palace of a foreign king. At the end of the conversation, the kakan-kakan report that they are ready to dress the Princess now, which gives the cue to the orchestra to begin the departure music. The Princess retires up the stairs and through the archway with her followers. This concludes the first of the stock scenes. It is interesting to note that in the old-fashioned traditional Gambuh companies, such as the one in Pedungan village, Badung Province, the women would never return to the stage after this scene.

Inevitably the second scene in the Gambuh performance introduces Panji, the male hero. This character is a typical Balinese type-character, the alus (refined) manis (sweet) leading man. Nowadays the role is often performed by a female dancer, as in Batuan village, Gianyar Province. The Panji has a distinguishing head-dress, which is decorated with fresh flowers, burning sticks of incense, dadap leaves, and pandanus blossoms. His voice is a high, monotonous falsetto, and he walks with a glide, crossing one leg before the other as he goes.

Before Panji appears, his attendants must be presented. First come a pair of portly ministers, the Demang and the Tumenggung, who dance as a pair; they perform a comic routine which is punctuated by loud, deep, stylized laughter. Their eyes bulge, which indicates them to be of the *keras* (strong) *kasar* (coarse) type, although they are on the side of the good party in the drama. The ministers call to each other as they dance: 'Hey, brother, don't stay too far away, come closer!' The comedy of their dancing is established in a fixed choreography which takes the dancers to each of the four corners of the kalangan to do comic animal movements in unison, in a burlesque idiom.

Once the comic ministers have finished their routine and are seated on the waiting mats, the *arya-arya* enter. This group of four dancers represents the army of the good party in the story, and is analogous to the kakan-kakan in the Putri scene. Later we shall see that the antagonist in the story has an equivalent group also. The arya-arya enter one by one and each one does a simple routine. Their steps are quite similar to those used in the Baris Gedé dances. As the arya-arya dance they call to one another: 'Hey, brother, come on! Get ready to meet King Panji!' Then they sit together on the mat with the other waiting ministers. Next the Old Prime Minister, or Patih Tua, appears; he is a refined old nobleman. His movement is similar to that of Panji, but is distinguished by a slight stiffness or awkwardness indicative of old age.

The Old Minister's voice is high, his bearing is dignified, his manner is grave. He dances down the entrance stairway and when he has introduced himself, he circles back to the foot of the stairs, where he calls for Panji to enter. The Prince joins him in the kalangan, and they dance together for a time. The duet is parallel to the dance of the Condong with the Putri.

When the five-minute duet has concluded, Panji returns to the top of the stairs, pausing for a time in the entrance archway. He dances what is considered to be the most difficult solo in Gambuh. Although the Condong must render a larger vocabulary of movement, the Panji has a more difficult problem of smooth linkage between isolated movement elements. And he must sing throughout, co-ordinating the phrasing of his chant perfectly with the phrasing of his gestures.

Panji is joined after a time by his servant, Semar, who will later serve as his interpreter. Semar is a coarse, comic type; he belongs to the servant class. He wears a simple Balinese cloth head-dress, often made of lucky checkered cloth instead of a

[38]

Javanese-style gelung. Semar dances a simple step. He holds his costume in one hand and extends the other forward, thumb up, in an ancient gesture of submission. His task as Panji nears the end of his introductory solo is to extend the proper traditional ceremonial greeting routine appropriate for a Balinese monarch. Semar compares Panji to the gods in beauty and wisdom and grace. He follows the Prince as he dances, begging his pardon, and beseeching the royal blessing. As they dance the men seated on the mats join by singing in chorus along with the gamelan.

This section is equivalent to the interaction of the Condong and Putri in the previous scene, and it finds an echo in the scene following in which the major antagonist will be presented. What is represented—the entrance of a noble character—is elaborated and ceremonialized. Dramatic time stands still while courtesies are extended and rituals of courtly etiquette are observed. Through Gambuh and other forms of dance-drama the Balinese have been able to preserve in detail a long tradition of formal courtly behaviour.

Once Panji has completed his lengthy entrance and has been properly received, the music and dance come to a halt. The courtiers are called from the resting mats by Semar, and they take their places in front of the Prince. Now a section of dialogue follows, called the *pegunem*, or meeting. The content of this scene will vary according to the plot of the particular story presented. Inevitably, however, the scene will progress in a certain way.

First, lengthy courtesies are exchanged: 'How are you? Why do you summon us today?' etc. After a while Panji comes to the central dramatic problem of the play. The assembled courtiers address their leader in unison, speaking in a chorus of voices pitched high, middle, and low. Panji replies in his high falsetto drawl, and Semar translates and interprets for the two groups, thus enabling the audience to understand the plot. During this section the Semar character is absolutely correct in his deportment and speaking—clowning is reserved for later in the performance.

Here is a specimen of dialogue from an early moment in a typical scene of this type:

Panji (in Kawi)

Uduh! My uncles are you all, my lords. I would now meet with you all together.

Semar (in High Balinese)

Aduh! My lords! My lord Panji is delighted to meet with you now. He has something important to discuss with you. Yes, with you, Uncle Demang, and with you, Uncle Tumenggung; oh yes, and with you also, sir, with you, the Venerable Adviser, and yes, he is pleased to meet with all of you, family members and soldiers all!

All Ministers (in Kawi)

Yes, yes, my lord, we are all prepared and happy to greet you. Please accept our respects and do not strike us with your dreadful curse.

Semar (in High Balinese)

My lord Panji, your Ministers greet you and offer their humble respects. They crave to know what task you have in mind for them today?

Panji (in Kawi)

Now I remember that my fiancée, Candra Kirana, has been lost in the forest of Gegelang and captured by the King of that country. News has come that he wants to marry her. Therefore I would have you accompany me to that country to bring her back again. Perhaps we will have to fight.

Semar (in High Balinese)

Ministers of King Panji, hearken to what the King has said! Now His Highness remembers that the love of his life, Princess Candra Kirana, has been kidnapped in the woods of Gegelang by its King. She is heartsick for love of Prince Panji and, therefore, we must go to help him to get her back. I'm afraid you'll have to fight, for the King of Gegelang is a dangerous fighter. Now you must gather food and weapons. Get the equipment, prepare to march for days! (Etc.)

[40]

The scene continues with a discussion of the particular method to be employed for the quest. Inevitably it will be decided that Panji is to go to the court of the foreign antagonist in disguise. Always there is an assumed identity or similar stratagem: in one Gambuh play Panji goes as a *dukun*, or folk doctor; in another, he is a dancer; in another, a shadow-puppeteer. The meeting scene concludes with the agreement by all the Ministers to Panji's proposed plan.

Now the dancer portraying Panji gives a signal to the game-lan, and the orchestra strikes up the music for the next subsection of the piece, which is called the *pangkat*, or formal departure. No matter what the particular incident of the story might be, there will usually be a formal departure at the end of the Panji scene. The characters form a line behind Panji and circle the kalangan a few times to represent travelling toward the foreign kingdom. The music may change as they walk along, to prepare for the mood of the scene to come.

This section also creates the opportunity for more modern Gambuh groups to introduce comic interludes. In Batuan a group of comic villagers and peasants called *bondres* characters appear during the pangkat. The travellers dispatch Semar to ask the idiotic rustics for directions. Predictably, the locals argue among themselves and cannot agree on the right direction to follow. When all seems hopeless, however, a friendly monkey appears and points out the way. Finally Panji and his followers leave by the steps, making their exit through the stone archway.

In the third scene of the typical Gambuh performance, the foreign antagonist King, called the Prabu, is introduced. His particular name varies according to the particular story. This scene is similar in structure to those which have preceded it. Before the Prabu may make his entrance his retinue of followers must be introduced and they must receive him with appropriate ceremony. The first minister to appear is Prabangsa. This character is of the 'rough' type. He is handsome, with a large moustache, protruding eyes, and a loud, low voice. Like all the principal characters, his gelung is decorated with flowers and burning sticks of incense that leave a fragrant trail of smoke

[41]

behind him wherever he goes on the stage. Prabangsa comes down into the kalangan and dances alone for a time, singing as he dances. Then he calls to his men, the *potet*, a comic group of soldiers who appear together at the top of the stairs.

The potet comes down into the kalangan to dance with their chief. Prabangsa leads them in a comic military formation routine, based on the drilling and manoeuvring of the Baris Gedé dances. Prabangsa switches from the Kawi language to ordinary Balinese, as he dispatches the potet in all directions, marching and counter-marching until they are in hopeless confusion. This scene is a great favourite with the children in the audience, who look forward to it impatiently through the long introductory passages of the performance.

The comic military routine lasts for ten minutes or so, before Prabangsa and his men take seats on the mats to rest. They are followed at once by the *kade-kadean*, or four heralds. These dancers enter in pairs and perform an intricate group dance with an elaborate choreography. They call to one another as they dance: 'Hey, brother! Come closer!' 'Get ready! Be prepared! The King is coming!' At the conclusion of their routine, the kade-kadean and the potet are brought to order by the Prabangsa to be ready for the entrance of the Prabu.

In contrast to the extended introductory solos performed by the Putri and Panji in their scenes, the Prabu dances only briefly and then moves quickly into the dialogue section of the scene. The Prabu is a 'strong' character, like Prabangsa, but he has his own way of moving, with arms held high to emphasize his pride. He laughs as he dances down into the midst of his waiting retinue, and sings a line or two from the Malat. He is followed by his *penasar* (buffoon), named Togog, who is the analogue to Panji's attendant, Semar. Like Semar, Togog received his name from Java, where these names are still used for comic servant characters in the *Wayang Kulit* (shadow-puppet) theatre.

The meeting in the Prabu's court moves the dramatic narrative forward. Very often, at this point in the development of the play a reason for bringing the disguised Panji into the court is established. For example, the King calls upon his ministers for advice after experiencing impotence when trying to consummate his union with Candra Kirana. The suggestion then comes forth that a dukun be summoned, to prescribe an appropriate medicine. And later in that disguise Panji comes into the Prabu's court.

In this rather typical variation of the plot, Panji appears at the conclusion of the meeting scene between the Prabu and his ministers. 'What is the reason for that commotion in the outer courtyard?' asks Prabu. Togog is sent to find out and is met by Semar. The two clowns then improvise a comic routine in rather vulgar Balinese. 'Who are you? What do you want?' asks Togog, after extended horseplay having little to do with the depicted situation. 'Let's see your identity card!' 'I didn't bring it with me,' Semar protests, 'Please don't add to my problems. I've got enough troubles!' 'What troubles?' demands Togog. 'I've got two dozen mouths to feed at home, and I don't know where to get rice to feed them all.' 'What's the matter? Don't you know about family planning?' is his reply, bringing laughs from the audience. The dialogue can grow quite *risqué*, to general merriment.

After a time the subject is brought around to the plot once more, and Semar reveals that his master is a dukun, very skilled at curing people with romantic problems. 'Just the thing! You must come to treat my master and his wives, especially the new one.' Thus Panji is admitted to the court, and the King explains his problem to the disguised Prince. 'I lose all desire when I approach my new wife, Candra Kirana. Help me, please.' Panji agrees to try, but he says that first he must interview the melancholy bride. Thus by a stratagem he gains admittance to her quarters.

In some villages the Gambuh performance includes a love scene, or *pengipuk*, which is performed by Panji and Putri at this point in the development of the action. The dance is in characteristic Gambuh style, but is probably a relatively recent addition, based on the love sequences in more modern dances. Panji and Putri circle each other flirtatiously, before—very slowly and gradually—coming close enough to touch. The Princess affects surprise that these advances are coming from a mere folk doctor and draws back, until Panji reveals his identity to her by dropping the white overskirt he has put on to indicate that he is impersonating a dukun. Their dance represents love-making in a highly conventionalized sequence of movements that is always restrained, and never loses decorum. But as the intensity of their wooing increases, Semar appears at the corner of the stage and burlesques the proceedings with graphic obscene witticisms and gestures.

In this juxtaposition of the vulgar with the sublime some essential basic ingredient of Balinese dance is clearly displayed: it is a pairing of the divine and the chthonic that asserts itself time and again in all the Balinese performing arts, as well as in the shadow-theatre and in literature.

Semar (in Low Balinese)

Aduh! Look at that! Delicious, yummy, yummy! (He pants and kisses one of the poles at the side of the kalangan, humping obscenely. Panji notices him and comes over to tap him on the shoulder, which brings him to his senses.) Sorry, boss, I just got carried away—I've been away from my wife too long! (Panji and Putri resume their cool and stylized love-making.)

After one or two episodes in which the intrigue of the drama is developed the play moves to its conclusion, which consists of a prolonged sequence of fighting scenes. Togog discovers the lovers at the conclusion of the pengipuk. 'Aduh, what's this? The dukun is making love to the Princess! Call the guard!' The stage is cleared and a series of highly-energetic mock-combats ensues, in which characters of equal rank are pitted against one another. The kade-kadean of Prabu square off against the arya-arya of Panji in a group combat drawn from Baris Gedé. Then the Prime Ministers of both sides contend in a duel, and finally Panji fights against the Prabu. Each of the episodes concludes with the victory of the good side. Between serious fighting sequences, which are carefully choreographed and highly pantomimic, there is a comic battle between Semar and Togog. The performance ends when at last the Prabu is defeated by Panji. The dancers may now retire, and the sacred gelung are returned to storage in a nearby structure in the jaba tengah with minor rituals to lay them away. The musicians may get up as well—the flutists have been blowing continuously for five or six hours or so.

We have described a representative 'typical' Gambuh performance above, but in fact there is much variation in practice among different villages and Gambuh clubs. In the most old-fashioned villages, as well as in villages with a shortage of female talent, the scenes involving the female characters are omitted. In others the first scene, with the Condong and Putri, is given, but the pengipuk is omitted, recalling the days perhaps when the dancers were all male. What is certain in any Gambuh performance is that there will be the meeting scene with Panji and his retinue, and there will also be a meeting with the Prabu and his retainers. There will be a pangkat, an intrigue involving Panji's disguise, at least one comic (bondres) scene, and the play will conclude with the obligatory sequence of battles. In addition to the possibility of a love scene, there is another optional stock scene, with established music, for weeping. These scenes are the elements from which Gambuh is made. A typical village group might have five or six different stories in its repertoire, but only forty minutes out of the complete six-hour performance would vary from story to story.

As we have mentioned earlier, Gambuh arose in the courtyards of the royal palaces of the Majapahit Empire, and in the courts of the Princes of the Balinese kingdoms that succeeded Majapahit.[6] The specific connection of the genre with the court was maintained down through the entire nineteenth century, when European travellers in Bali were entertained with performances of Gambuh while visiting Balinese nobles on diplomatic business.[7] The Gambuh troupes described by these travellers were all male, with pre-adolescent boys trained to play the female roles. Performances of Gambuh do not seem to have been limited to special ritual occasions. The nobleman sponsored a Gambuh group, either in the palace itself, or in a convenient nearby village. When distinguished guests arrived to visit, or when the Prince wished to divert himself and his family, the group was sent for. Performances were also given in connection with the religious festivals, as part of the nobleman's contribution to the event.

When Bali finally came under Dutch control in the early years of this century, the power of the nobility was to a great extent checked, and many of the former ruling families were reduced in circumstances. Patronage of the arts by the upper-caste families did not cease altogether immediately after the Dutch conquest, but it gradually diminished in scale all over Bali, and large retinues of artists, musicians, and dancers were no longer supported behind palace walls.

It was necessary for the villages themselves to take up responsibility for the support of the Gambuh groups. Performances given by the players had come to be considered an indispensable element at a successful major village Odalan. Certain particularly wealthy villages with strong Gambuh traditions were able to take on the responsibility. In some villages, such as Batuan, Gianyar Province, certain families traditionally had provided most of the Gambuh dancers, and keeping the form alive was therefore a matter of clan as well as village responsibility. In many places, however, Gambuh disappeared early in the twentieth century.

Gambuh declined in importance among the traditional dance varieties during the 1920s and 1930s. It was all but abandoned in the enthusiasm for new forms generated by a great renaissance that occurred in all the Balinese arts after the First World War. By the mid-1930s a European observer noted that Gambuh was on the verge of extinction, performed only rarely in a few very traditional villages.[8] He reported that the performance was given without any real interest or enthusiasm. It had declined to a mere formality, possessing only a vestigial remnant of its former importance and was preserved merely out of respect for its antiquity and its still potent associations with the palaces.

Since the end of the Second World War, however, and especially in the last decade, Gambuh has taken on new life. Several

[46]

old groups have been revived, and new ones have been started. Scholars and artists associated with government schools and other institutions have been important in drawing Balinese attention to this treasure of the island's heritage. Gambuh style and technique have been added to the curriculum of ASTI, the Dance Academy in Denpasar. At present approximately a dozen groups are active in Bali, supported entirely by the villages or wards to which the members belong.

Like many Balinese performing arts groups, the Gambuh clubs are voluntary associations, formed for the essential purpose of contributing to the worship at the village temple. Most of the village performers are not professional dancers and have other primary occupations. The training of the group is conducted not by a professional dance teacher—as would have been the case in the palace a century ago—but by the older dancers who remember how the performance was done when they were younger.

In recent years, with the opening of the *Wredhi Budaya* Arts Center in Denpasar, a stage has been created where secular performances of Gambuh can once again take place. Condensed versions of the dance-drama have been created by groups from Batuan and Pedungan, as well as by dancers at the Dance Academy (ASTI-Bali). In these shorter performances, intended to appeal to a general audience of Balinese and foreign visitors, dramatic values have been re-emphasized and the narrative element has been heightened. Repetitious sections of choreography have been cut and condensed, and the dancers are more carefully trained, with a renewed emphasis on skill, polish and consistency. In the case of Gambuh, in fact, it would seem that modernization in the Balinese context involves a return to a very old set of traditional values—those of the sophisticated courtiers of the Majapahit Empire.[9]

1. Stutterheim (1935), pp. 6—25.

2. Suleiman (1974), *passim*.

3. Hanna (1976), and Boon (1977), pp. 1—90, provide some accounts of early contacts between Bali and the West.

4. Holt (1967), pp. 281—9; various Balinese Babad manuscripts are on deposit in Listibya Library, Denpasar. They are similar in nature to Berg's (1929).

5. Bandem (1972); Bandem and deBoer (1978).

6. See also Ras (1973).

7. Jacobs (1883), pp. 91—2, is a good example of an account by a Dutch official traveller who was entertained by Gambuh.

8. Spies (1936), p. 59.

9. Robson (1971), pp. 85—91, describes court Gambuh through the eyes of a Majapahit-era poet.

3 Masked Dances of the *Bebali* Group

Two masked dance genres of great importance in Balinese culture belong to the bebali category of sacred dances: Topeng Pajegan and Wayang Wong. The genres to be considered in this chapter are dramatic dances and share with Gambuh an association with Hinduized court culture. But Wayang Wong and Topeng are later developments than Gambuh and are products not of the Hindu-Javanese courts of the sixteenth-century Majapahit Empire but of the seventeenth- and eighteenth-century Hindu-Balinese courts which evolved in the capital cities of Gel-gel and Klungkung.

These dance genres were created by artists who explicitly set out to establish new forms. Devised in the great central palace of the Balinese capital city, Topeng Pajegan and Wayang Wong were disseminated to the lesser satellite courts in such larger settlements as Badung, Bangli, Gianyar and others. The creation and propagation of these forms were associated with particular families of sponsors and artists, and the all-important masks and head-dresses employed in the performance have been handed down in particular families, acquiring with each generation greater magical quality, or *pasupati*. In addition to the sanctity lent by great age alone, these treasures have often been additionally charged with power by means of magical inscriptions.

Many categories of the sacred in Bali can become relevant to the arts: there are sacred gestures, sacred syllables, sacred images, sacred places, sacred melodies, sacred clothing, sacred weapons, and other sacred objects. The sacral quality, called *těngět*, inheres in the specific object, locale, etc., and is particular, definite and fixed. Unlike the doll-like pratima which are only temporarily inhabited by the visiting deities at an Odalan, a sacred kris (dagger), for example, or a sacred mask, has its power on a permanent basis. And that power is handed down from generation to generation within a particular clan. The heirlooms that are těngět both literally embody and symbolically represent the family's sustaining power, a power which is both displayed and replenished from time to time by appropriate reconsecration and public presentation of the objects. The

[49]

use of at least one sacred mask and/or head-dress is an essential part of every bebali performance.

Masked dancing has been known on Bali for more than a millennium. The Berutuk masks as well as many native-Balinese animal masks are quite similar in style to masks found on other islands of the Indonesian archipelago, such as the *Topeng Hudoq* of East Kalimantan (Borneo), as well as to masks used in dances of various groups in Sulawesi (Celebes) and Irian Jaya (West New Guinea). None of the surviving Balinese dance forms employing masks of this type makes use of a developed narrative or story, although rudimentary dramatic features are occasionally present in them.

Our oldest record of masked dance on Bali dates to the copperplate charter *Praçasti Bebetin* (A.D. 896), inscribed during the reign of King Ugrasena of Bedulu.[1] The charter lists masked dancers (*partapukan*) along with other court artists, servants and functionaries. The charter is inscribed in the Old Javanese language, showing that Hindu influence had already reached the island by this time. Unfortunately we know nothing of the nature of the dances performed by these ancient civil servants. The earliest descriptive accounts we have of Balinese masked dances are given in the considerably later Panji stories, such as *Malat* and *Wangbang Wedeya*, and concern forms of dance quite similar in nature to Gambuh.[2]

The making of masks in modern Bali retains many traditional features, at least with respect to masks intended for use in performance rather than for sale at the tourist shop. The mask-maker is a special kind of artisan, who must be consecrated to his calling in a special ceremony. The craft most often passes down in specific families. The maker must know the necessary prayers and ceremonies connected with masks and an entire code of ritual lore, the *Dharmaning Sangging*, which applies to the maker.

Making a magically-powerful mask commences with the selection of the wood from a potent tree growing in a sacred place. The graveyard tree (*pohon kepuh*) or the tree in the village *Pura Dalem* (death temple) is propitiated with prayers and offerings before a mask-sized slab is cut from the living wood of its trunk. The wood is soaked in water for a few days and then is set aside for several seasons to dry before it can be carved. The first cut made by the mask-maker is accompanied by an appropriate little ritual, and another ceremony is given when the mask has been finished. A magic letter is written on the interior face of the mask at that time, and it is taken to a sacred place, along with a large offering. There spirits are invited to enter the mask, while the future users and the mask-maker watch from a safe distance. It is said that often the power enters the mask visibly, in the form of a glowing nimbus like St. Elmo's fire. Then the mask is ready for use in the bebali dances. Not all of the masks will have had this special treatment, but there will always be at least one of them in a bebali performance. In Gambuh it is the gelung (head-dresses) which are thus infused with magical power.

Topeng Pajegan

On the narrow road leading from Denpasar to Gianyar, above the River Petanu, is located the lovely old Balinese village of Blah-batuh. This prosperous community with rich ricelands has a large population of families who were until the late nineteenth century associated with the court of the paramount Balinese kingdom, located first in Gel-gel and later moved to Klungkung. One of these families, a *ksatrya*-caste clan called the *Pemaksan Gusti Ngurah Jelantik*, maintains its principal temple in Blah-batuh, and in that temple, the *Pura Penataran Topeng*, is kept an especially sacred collection of palm-leaf manuscripts, wayang puppets, and topeng (masks). The word 'topeng' comes from the root 'tup', meaning 'cover', and refers to something pressed against the face, i.e., a mask. The term is used specifically to denote the masks used in the genre of dance-drama called To-peng. The masks kept in Blahbatuh are heirlooms belonging to the Jelantik family, and they are said to be the oldest topeng in Bali.

The masks themselves, which are now regarded as too sacred to photograph, are of two types. The first type, and probably the

[51]

oldest, is represented by six masks covering the full face with a mouthpiece on the inside of the mask which provides a means for the dancer to hold it while dancing. This method of holding a mask between clenched teeth is still seen today in Sunda (West Java) and in Central Java, but it is not used at all on Bali. The remaining masks, fifteen in number, are more similar in style to modern Balinese masks; they are held to the dancer's face by means of an elastic band. This group was probably made by native craftsmen inspired by the six imported examples.

The collection of sacred *lontar* manuscripts kept together with the old masks and puppets includes a legendary-historical account of the Jelantik clan, from its founding in the time of Dalem (King) Batu Renggong (A.D. 1460–1550) to the year 1779, when the clan moved from Klungkung to Blahbatuh. This account, called the *Babad Blahbatuh*, recounts history from the point of view of the family, emphasizing its exploits, and tracing its lineage. Little attention is given to peripheral matters. But it presents an account of how Topeng Pajegan came to Bali that seems as likely as any we might imagine.

According to the manuscript, Dalem Batu Renggong sent an expedition in the late sixteenth century to attack the East Javanese kingdom of Blambangan, under the leadership of his two War Ministers, Patih Ularan and Patih Jelantik, the founder of the present Blahbatuh Jelantik line. The Balinese invasion succeeded in sacking the palace of the King of Blambangan, although Jelantik was killed in the battle. Patih Ularan brought home the basket of masks as booty, and he displayed them to the King in Gel-gel as proof that the expedition had succeeded. The treasures were then stored in the palace treasury, where they lay unused for a century.

Descendants of the first Jelantik followed their illustrious ancestor into the service of the Kings of Bali, and often served in the position of Patih (Prime Minister). Sometime during the reign of Dalem Batu Renggong's grandson, Dalem Dimadé, between 1665 and 1686, Patih I Gusti Pering Jelantik composed a dance-drama and the captured masks were used for the first time in the premiere performance in Bali of Topeng Pajegan.

[52]

Following this it became customary for the masks to be used in performance every six months, on the occasion of Odalan in the palace, at first in Gel-gel and later in Klungkung, when the court moved there about A.D. 1715. The manuscript ends with the report that the masks were taken to Blahbatuh when, as a result of political intrigue and a *coup* in the court of Klungkung, the Jelantik family went into exile to lands they held in the Blahbatuh area. The family survived the transition to Dutch colonial rule and later to life under the independent government of Indonesia with little loss of power or prestige. Members of the family are still active patrons of the performing arts, and especially of Topeng.

Alone among the dances classified as Bebali, Topeng Pajegan contains embedded ritual aspects similar to those of the wali dances described in the first chapter. In fact Topeng Pajegan is sometimes known as *Topeng Wali*. At an Odalan the performance is given therefore in the jeroan, which is the most sacred part of the temple. But temple festivals are not the only events calling for a performance of Topeng Pajegan: weddings, cremations, tooth-filings and other ceremonies taking place within the family circle are also highly appropriate occasions. The dancer serves in either situation as both priest and entertainer and thus works in the most sacred area available. When performing in a private household compound he dances in the *sanggah*, or family temple. In either location the dancer presents a small offering and pours a libation to consecrate the ground for his performance. The main ritual will take place later, after the conclusion of the story.

The distinguishing aspect of Topeng Pajegan is that it is a monodrama. The single dancer tells a story by portraying a succession of masked characters, one after the other. The word 'Pajegan' comes from terminology used in purchasing rice: when someone buys a crop of paddy as a whole he is said to *majeg* the crop. With the help of a few simple theatrical conventions the soloist is able to tell an intricate and engrossing story. Topeng Pajegan is by far the most dramatic of the bebali dance forms; in none of the others are the intricacies of the narrative of much interest to either dancer or audience.

The stories presented in Topeng are always taken from the chronicles of Balinese history and deal with the semi-legendary feats of the Hindu-Balinese kings and their ministers. The dancer composes his own plays from the manuscript sources according to the traditional procedures. The story presented on a particular occasion is chosen by the dancer according to the needs and desires of the sponsor. The story of the expedition whereby the first Patih Jelantik attacked Blambangan under the orders of Dalem Batu Renggong is itself a popular subject in the repertoire.[3]

The ritual aspect is not mixed in with the story-telling but is reserved for the very end. In a sense all the rest of the performance is a prologue to the ritual. At the end, regardless of what story has been presented, a strange white-faced, buck-toothed, smiling character with long, wild hair comes to the stage. His name is Sidha Karya, which means 'The one who can do the task'. When he is wearing this mask (and only then) the dancer serves a specifically priestly function.

The playing space for the performance is a small oval area on the bare earth, some 8 by 12 feet in size. The dancer sets his basket of masks in front of the gamelan gong which will accompany him; usually there is no curtain. His playing is oriented in the direction toward the shrine where the gods are sitting invisibly to watch. During the performance his masks are spread out on a small table and a straight-backed chair is near at hand for use as needed.

The performance invariably begins with the presentation of a group of three introductory character studies (*pengelembar*) which give the performer the opportunity to demonstrate his skill as a dancer; once the performance begins there will be few opportunities to interrupt the story with extended passages of pure dancing. These characters have no connection to the story. The first introductory character is always the Patih; he is a character of the strong and crude type. His face is red, indicating that he is brave and easily angered. His movements are broad, and extended; they convey strong tension. This character and the other pengelembar demonstrate a mood of wonder and astonishment, as if suddenly wrenched from the distant past into the world of the present.

The red-faced Patih is followed by two additional masks, chosen by the dancer. Often another Patih will be presented, with a brown face and big moustache; his movement is rather comic in quality and very vigorous. A final introductory mask depicts a comic yet dignified old gentleman, known as the *Tua*. Each of these dances begins with a particular set of movements known as *mungkah lawang*, or 'opening the door'. Although the dancer makes use of no curtain at all in the usual Topeng Pajegan performance, these first movements represent pantomimically the shaking of a curtain. In the ensemble Topeng performance called *Topeng Panca*, an actual curtain is employed, which is shaken vigorously before a new character enters the stage for the first time. This is similar to the 'curtain look' seen in the Kathakali dance-drama of South India, and may have descended from an ancient Indian source. In recent years the use of the curtain has also become quite common in Topeng Pajegan.

Story-telling in Topeng Pajegan takes place according to a firmly established set of conventions. The basic framework is similar to that employed in Gambuh. The dancer generally alternates the full-face masks of high-born and noble characters with the half-masks allowing speech, which are worn by the servants and comic peasant (bondres) characters. The kings and noblemen convey their meaning in gesture, while the attendants may speak for their masters in Kawi or for themselves in Balinese. Occasional dissociation of voice and body is a striking and exotic aspect of the story-telling mode of the genre: at times the dancer will bend his body in cringing subordination in keeping with his role as palace servant, while from his lips come the imperious commands in Kawi of his invisible master.

The language employed in Topeng Pajegan is a rich and varied medium of literary and theatrical expression. A ranked series of levels ranging from the most sacred (at the kaja end of the linguistic spectrum) to the demonic and obscene (at the kelod extreme) is employed. The top level, used only for prayers, is Sanskrit. Beneath it are quotations from the Kawi literary classics in verse; these are invariably sung and are introduced at appropriate places in the action to lend majesty and dignity to the moment. Somewhat lower yet on the scale is the prose Kawi spoken by the high-ranked characters of the drama. In practice, since these characters usually wear full-face masks, the Kawi is spoken *for* these characters by their servants. The penasar (retainers) themselves use the 'high' Balinese when addressing their masters, and ordinary vernacular Balinese when addressing the audience or other low-ranking people. *Bali kasar*, 'low' Balinese, is not a complete language but consists of vulgar terms and expressions considered quite shocking in everyday life. It is used in the performance only by the bondres characters and servants who taunt and insult the enemy as the drama moves toward its violent climax.

As in the Gambuh dance-drama, action in Topeng Pajegan is built in a series of stock scenes occurring in a predictable order. After the pengelembar have been presented the dancer begins to relate the particulars of the chosen tale. This is invariably begun by the penasar, who is a descendant of the character Semar from the older Gambuh form. The penasar appears in many of the more modern genres of dance-drama, serving as attendant to the major characters. In Topeng the penasar can be of two different types, either the *Penasar Kelihan* (the 'older brother'), or the *Penasar Cenikan* (the 'younger brother'). In multi-player Topeng Panca these penasar always appear in a pair, working as a comic team; the older brother serves as straight man to the antics of the younger. In Topeng Pajegan the two servants alternate in delivering the exposition of the play.

The penasar begins his scene with singing and a comic dance. Then he establishes the exposition of the story to follow. The Penasar Kelihan is often given the character name 'Punta'. He speaks with a low voice, and has a half-mask that is brown in colour, furnished with a large black moustache and bulging eyes. The following indicates the nature of his first monologue:

Punta (singing in Kawi)

When the Five Pandawas rose up at dawn
Departing from the city of Wirata,
Like the rising sun were they
Gleaming over the whole world.

Ho, ho, ho, ha, ha, ha! Lordy, me! I'm so happy to be the chief
servant here in the palace of Gel-gel, great capital city of ancient
Bali! My master Dalem Batu Renggong is going to arrive soon,
here in the beautiful audience chamber. What a mighty king is
he, my master! His power is known over the whole world.

His people are happy, his lands are at peace—why, we have a
wonderful standard of living, with low taxes, no inflation, and
plenty of coconuts for export! And you know, I'm also happy for
another reason. My boss, King Batu Renggong, has a terrific
Patih, a mighty Prime Minister, doughty in battle, named I Gusti
Ngurah Jelantik. There's supposed to be an audience held today,
and I can't imagine what is going to happen . . .

The penasar continues until the basic background to the story
is clear. He may also embellish the exposition with jokes that are
relevant to the story and its theme.

The second character to appear in a Topeng performance is the
King. In the story begun in the example given above his name
would be Dalem Batu Renggong; in another tale he would have a
different identity. The mask of the King is of the refined type,
and covers the full face. The dancer must therefore perform in
silence when portraying this character. The mask of the *Dalem*,
as the type is known, is always white or very light green; slight
variations in appearance distinguish the masks of different
regional traditions, but the basic iconography is immediately
recognizable no matter where the performance is given. The
face represented on the mask is an idealized portrait, representing kings as a class rather than any specific individual.

The scene presenting the Dalem follows a fixed traditional
format, commencing with an extended dance routine that
demonstrates the prototypical qualities of Hindu-Balinese
kingship: dignity, grace, beauty, and refinement. This solo is a

set-piece and is used whenever the Dalem first appears, regardless of the story.

Only after his lengthy approach does the Dalem enter the specific context of the tale. The music accompanying his entrance is brought to a quick transition by an abrupt and commanding clap of the dancer's hands. Now he will begin the second part of the scene, in which pantomime rather than pure dance is the means of expression. This section is quite short and also follows an established scheme. The King indicates alertness and then shows that he is seeing someone approach; with a gesture he beckons the visitor to come closer.

At this point the dancer leaves the stage, although the King's presence remains there, invisible. During the following scene another character will enter, to advance the story. Often he will be a messenger. In any case the character will wear a half-mask, permitting speech. The dancer speaks Kawi to represent the speech of the King, alternating with 'high Balinese' spoken by the lower-ranking character. During this section of the performance a mission or attack of some kind is usually ordered.

The second character leaves the stage at the conclusion of the audience scene. Now when the dancer returns, as one or another of the penasar characters, he can improve the audience's understanding of the dramatic situation and perhaps do a little clowning as well. The stance of the penasar is basically comic throughout the play, but he is always respectful of his masters. At this point in the story the penasar must prepare for the entrance of the next essential character, the strong, good Patih, whose function is always to carry out the will of the refined King.

In Topeng the refined King is never represented doing anything so undignified as fighting: mysterious, almost insubstantial, he is half-way between common men and the gods themselves. His Patih however is a man of action as well as good breeding. He is the quintessential ksatrya (knightly) warrior. His face is brown, his eyes are large, and he has a fierce moustache. In some of the Patih masks the teeth are bared, while in others the lips are closed. His movement is energetic and forceful yet always retains control and an overall sense of dignity. The characterization might seem familiar, and indeed it is, for the good Patih has received his vocabulary of movement and general appearance from the character Prabangsa in the Gambuh. There this character is a minister for the antagonistic King, but with no change in basic appearance he becomes the active protagonist in Topeng.

The Patih has his own introductory dance solo, demonstrating the qualities of his character. Then he gestures to his (invisible) penasar to make ready for departure on the planned expedition, the nature of which depends on the particular tale presented.

In the next section of the play a succession of comic characters, or bondres is presented. These characters belong to the lower caste and are very eccentric. They often represent oppressed villagers who need the services of the Patih to rescue them from distress. In the presentation of bondres the comic virtuosity of the dancer is tested and demonstrated. He impersonates a gallery of comic personages, perhaps a half-dozen in all. The audience looks forward eagerly to this section, which exists in different forms in most of the genres of Balinese dance-drama. Many of the bondres are portrayed as suffering from physical defects and handicaps; in fact one medical scholar used a group of bondres masks to discuss common genetic defects found on the island.[4] Some characters have buck teeth, others have cleft palates; still others have long noses or no nose at all; some are represented as being blind or deaf, or as stutterers. The Balinese audience enjoys slapstick humour, to which these characters lend themselves very well. The jokes occasionally have a rather cruel edge.

The final character appears after the last of the bondres. This is the antagonist King, who very often is the possessor of supernatural powers. His mask is yellow or red; he has a moustache and large eyes. His appearance is often bestial. Visible fangs may protrude from his mouth. The antagonist King wears a characteristic gelung, similar to the head-dress worn by the Prabu, who is his counterpart in Gambuh. Very often his mask has an open mouth, which permits at least limited speech. This King enters the stage quickly; he does not have an extended solo. As he appears dramatic tension begins to rise, for the audience knows that when he comes into view the end of the story is near. He comes out talking and gesturing excitedly—it is clear that his country is being attacked; he orders his followers to make ready and he then departs.

Once more the Patih appears, to the insistent pounding of *Gending Batel* played on the gamelan. The Patih mimics a great hand-to-hand struggle, in which he battles against his (invisible) opponent, the antagonist King. This section comes to a quick conclusion as the dancer works his way up to his table of masks and then holds the face of the villain aloft, in token of the victory of the Patih and the beheading of the antagonist. A moment later one of the penasar appears and explains that the story is over, that the enemy has been defeated, and that it is now time for a celebration. The narrative portion of the performance is ended, and it is time for the ritual to begin.

At this time the dancer puts on the mask of Sidha Karya, along with a wig with long and wild hair. The priest has already said prayers over the offering before the dancer seizes it and dances with it over to the shrine, shouting and laughing and praying in Sanskrit over the bowl of fruit and flowers. He gestures with the sacred mudra used by the priests when they pray. Once he has presented the offering to the gods he turns back and showers the audience with handfuls of specially blessed *kepeng* kept with the offering. The spectators scramble to pick up the lucky money. Sidha Karya distributes the lucky tokens. To bless the spectators further he sprinkles holy water and flings rice in their direction.

Suddenly while distributing these blessings Sidha Karya lunges into the audience and snatches up one of the small children who make up a large part of the crowd. All of the youngsters in the audience have been waiting for this moment and rush here and there, shrieking with fright as he approaches, but the dancer always seems to be able to catch one. He carries the struggling child over to the shrine and holds him up to the gods before giving him a small present from the offerings there.

[60]

The child is then put down and disappears back into the crowd with his trophy. The performance is over, for now the ritual is complete. The members of the audience/congregation now can approach the shrine for individual prayers. The dancer puts away his masks in its basket after presenting a small offering to the god Wisnumurti, Patron of Dance. He is ready to return to his own village.

Unlike the performers of Gambuh and of the wali dances, the dancer of Topeng Pajegan is not necessarily a member of the group celebrating the occasion for which his services are required. In fact it is more usual for the dancer to be engaged for the event on a professional basis. Few villages could hope to number a person with all the special qualifications required for the demanding Topeng Pajegan among their inhabitants. Like the mask-maker the Topeng dancer needs to know a special code of his craft, the *Bebali Sidha Karya*, which prescribes prayers and offerings and behavioural taboos to be followed by the performer. In addition, the Topeng dancer must be able to read the *Babad*, or historical chronicles, from which his stories are made, and he must be able to dramatize his own material from the bare outlines of events given in the source. Comic ability is also a specific requirement, as is the ability to improvise in a number of characters. The dancer must also be able to sing and to chant lengthy passages of Kawi poetry from memory. And by no means least, he must be a talented dancer.

Before a dancer may give his first performance of Topeng Pajegan he must undergo a consecration ceremony in which he is confirmed in the profession. Thereafter he may perform at temple festivals in his own village or at events sponsored within his own clan. If some measure of fame is achieved locally, he may then be called by other villages or kin-groups to perform on their behalf. The payment for these professional engagements is quite modest—in 1978 it consisted of a fee of about US$10 for the entire performance, plus the left-over offering. At the present time no more than a dozen performers of Topeng Pajegan are still active in Bali.

In recent years, there has been a renaissance of interest among the larger Balinese clans in questions of their roots and origins. Many groups that have not had heirloom copperplate charters or historical Babad manuscripts have commissioned new ones to reinforce new perceptions of the group's historical prestige and influence. In the wake of this development has also come a new set of opportunities for the performers of Topeng Pajegan, for hand in hand with the new commissions for written historical documents has come the desire to see the story of the kin-group's origin enacted, visualized for the clan by a Topeng Pajegan dancer. Some of the dancers in fact do double duty, composing the newly 'discovered' lontar manuscript in the daytime and performing a Topeng play taken from it that night. This kind of effort is work for a truly well-educated scholar and multi-talented artist.

Interlude: Barong Kedingkling

It is told in the village of Madangan, Gianyar Province, of a terrible pestilence that threatened the people about 250 years ago, when King Batu Renggong's great-grandson was on the throne in Klungkung. The new King's elder brother, I Dalem Agung Pemayun, was driven into exile after he had refused to assume the title of King of Bali himself. After I Dalem Agung Pemayun had wandered for some time in the wilderness of the northern mountain district and meditated there, he travelled to the south and entered Madangan while the epidemic was raging. The desperate villagers appealed to the great man for help, and he proposed a possible remedy for their distress. 'In the palace in Klungkung are some wonderfully powerful sacred masks', he told them. 'They represent the sacred monkeys of the holy *Ramayana*, and they have the power to drive out disease.' I Dalem Agung Pemayun told the people of ceremonies conducted in the palace to protect against disease by driving out the buta, and at his suggestion the villagers made a series of nine masks, copies of the masks in the Klungkung palace, and inaugurated a wali dance called *Barong Kedingkling* to protect themselves against disease. The ceremony is still performed in

[62]

the village every six months at one of the village temples, the Pura Dalem Madangan. There, too, the old masks are kept between festivals.

Barong Kedingkling is similar to rituals performed in several other Balinese villages, where the form may be called *Barong Belasbelasan*. 'Barong' is a general Balinese term for a mask representing a mythological animal or supernatural being; 'kedingkling' means 'hopping', while *'belasbelasan'* means 'going in separate directions'.

The event begins at noon in the jeroan of the temple. The leader of the dancers, wearing a very handsome mask in the style of Wayang Wong (see below) and a costume made of white palm fibres, has the name Sugriwa, King of the Monkeys, in the old epic. He enters the inner courtyard of the temple, dancing to the accompaniment of a simple percussion orchestra, the *gamelan batel*. He carries an ornately worked silver tray, on which are arranged bits of roast pork (*babi guling*, a well-loved culinary specialty of the Gianyar Province). His dance is very simple, without rigorous technical demands, and is based on mimicry of monkey movement. This role is usually performed by an ordained pemangku. Sugriwa dances about in the jeroan, singing a Balinese song, and then he calls in his two Patih, Anoman and Anggada. The two apes are masked and costumed like their King, but they are dressed in different colours: Anoman wears white; Anggada wears red. They carry a live pig hanging upside-down from a pole which they carry between them. This animal will be sacrificed later, at the conclusion of the ceremony.

Anoman and Anggada are followed into the jeroan by four additional monkeys, each bearing a different kind of offering on a plate. They are accompanied by two characters belonging to the general category of penasar, or comic attendants. This particular pair of retainers is Twalen and his son Wredah, who are very popular characters in several important genres of Balinese dance and theatre. Found in all plays that derive from the *Ramayana* and *Mahabharata* epics, they serve as helpers, counsellors and jesters for the characters of the good party.

Twalen and Wredah serve King Sugriwa in Barong Keding-kling. They interpret his commands into Balinese from Kawi so that the audience can understand what he and the other monkeys are saying, and they explain the ritual to the watchers as well. They comment on the action of the simple 'play' that is to be performed. Twalen and Wredah carry incense and holy water and dance together with the seven monkeys in the inner courtyard. The choreographic pattern and the dancing are very simple.

With a shouted signal, the Monkey King calls his band together to form a circle in the middle of the courtyard. All sit as Sugriwa exercises a pemangku's function in presenting the offerings to the pelinggih. The pig and the other meat offerings are kept to one side, for they will be presented later, to the buta rather than to the gods. Sugriwa's troupe sits quietly for half an hour or so as the offerings are presented. Then they rise, and with loud shouts and monkey noises rush out of the jeroan to visit all the households in the village individually.

The monkeys swarm about the town singly and in pairs, while the gamelan is picked up and moved to the central street. There the musicians continue to add to the general din. The clamour is intense; children rush to and fro, and the monkeys swarm into every household. Once inside the compound the monkey visits the sanggah (house temple) and climbs any coconut or fruit trees that grow on the property.

Twalen and Wredah carry holy water from house to house. They act as traffic wardens for the monkeys, directing them where to go. The older dancers who have begun the ceremony pass on their masks to younger men who take turns in the game. Bold and naughty 'monkeys' will sometimes rob the kitchens of the households they visit; everywhere people give them small presents of food and money.

The special affinity of the monkey for the productive trees of the village is a central aspect of the performance. Each tree is climbed and shaken to drive off vexing spirits. The squirrel population of the village—alarmed by the tree-climbers—flees, squawking in protest. In this manner the buta are also driven

[64]

out of the private homes in the village into the public streets, where they can be bribed with offerings and then sent on their way out of town.

At about six o'clock in the evening, the dancers gather once again in the inner temple. The forty or so who have taken part are nearly exhausted from the running and hopping and climbing and shouting they have done. Now the pig and five chickens are sacrificed and arranged in an elaborate offering to the buta which is placed on the ground. The demons are then told to go away, and the way has been prepared for a successful Odalan, which will begin the next day with a performance of Baris Gedé or Rejang. The old monkey masks are returned to their storage place in the temple until the next Odalan.

Variations on this ritual performance can be found in many Balinese villages in versions of the form that are more or less complex. The rite is one of a very large number of ceremonies still practised on the island involving the expulsion of buta. Before the Balinese New Year (*Hari Nyepi*), many villages expel the buta with noise and offerings. Sometimes young men fight with burning torches as a feature of these events. In the Barong Kedingkling we see once again a manifestation of the connection in Bali between dancing and exorcism, with ritual power attached to the actual implements (in this case the masks) used in the performance.

Wayang Wong

According to Madangan legend, the sacred masks belonging to the Barong Kedingkling rite were copied from a collection of masks kept in the palace of the King of Klungkung, where they had been kept (but not used in performance) since time immemorial. The original set of court masks may very well survive today, in the village of Kamasan, Klungkung Province, which long provided servants and artisans to the royal palace. A group of fine old masks is kept in the *Pura Penataran*, which is the principal temple for the Pulasari clan, a family long prominent in court circles, especially during the nineteenth century. According to members of the family, the masks and musical instruments and other cultural treasures were brought to the temple at the time of the destruction of the palace of Klungkung by the Dutch in 1908.

Fifteen masks are in this collection. Although it is not clear that all are equally old, they are carved and painted in a very characteristic style, which is noticeably different from the style employed by the makers of topeng. They resemble other old Balinese masks representing fantastic or mythical animals. The faces are large, with prominent ears that are decorated with *rumbing*, a particular kind of ear ornament. Behind the masks the *sekar taji*, a kind of gilded leather ornamental collar, is worn; this is an indispensable part of the costume. These masks are very similar to the mask worn by the *Barong Ket*, which we shall discuss in a later chapter. Their style shows Chinese influence and would seem to be very old. In many villages the pratima into which the gods descend at an Odalan are guarded by small carved companion figures, called 'lions', with faces carved and painted in this same distinctive manner.

Dalem Gedé Kusamba was King of Klungkung between 1775 and 1825. According to the *Babad Dalem*, a legendary history of the kings of Gel-gel and Klungkung, Dalem Gedé Kusamba ordered his chief dancers to create a new form of dramatic dance using the royal collection of sacred masks.[5] He stipulated that the repertoire for the new genre was to be taken from the *Ramayana*, and he directed that the dancers were to create a Wayang Wong, that is a dance based on the Wayang (shadow-puppet) theatre using men in place of puppets. The resulting form that his artists created acquired the name Wayang Wong, by which it is known today. The genre is distinct from the dramatic dance of the same name which exists in Central Java, although some of the ideas behind the two genres are similar.

The *Ramayana* epic, which was to provide the basis for Wayang Wong, has been known and admired in Bali at least since the tenth century. It was inscribed in palm-leaf manuscripts which have been passed down and faithfully re-copied from generation to generation until the present-day. No work of

Hindu literature is better known on Bali than the *Ramayana*, and certain characters from it, especially the White Monkey Anoman, are beloved popular favourites among Balinese children. The text of the poem known on the island is written in the Kawi language; it has long had a scriptural significance for the Balinese people, and reading aloud from it is considered to be an act of devotion. Clubs (*Seka Mabasan*) exist for the purpose of reading (that is chanting) aloud from the *Ramayana* and other classics. Recitations by these groups are an indispensable part of nearly every Balinese religious celebration.[6]

The *Ramayana* also provided an important source of subject matter for traditional Balinese painters, many of whom were attached to the royal court in Klungkung.[7] Today the Pulasari family, holders of the Kamasan masks, is still known for its painters of *Ramayana*. Performances of Wayang Wong have been another traditional way by which the old epic has been preserved and reinvigorated with meaning for successive generations of Balinese. Until this century in fact Wayang Wong was the only form of dance-drama in which episodes from the *Ramayana* were presented.

The direction to the choreographers that the *Ramayana* be taken for subject matter was especially apt, in the light of the old exorcist associations accompanying masks of the Wayang Wong type. The *Ramayana* story lends itself very well to ceremonies for frightening or otherwise driving away buta, for the epic tells of the defeat of the King of the buta (Rawana) along with his entire army of ogres and imps. The good party in the story furthermore is made up for the most part of 'monkeys', who are the followers of the hero Ramadewa. These 'monkeys' are no mere simians— many of them are hybrid creatures resulting from intermarriage of a monkey with a tiger, for example, or a bird, or a cow. The monkeys in Wayang Wong are mythical beings; in them ancient Balinese protectors in the form of benevolent mythical animals survive in thin disguise.

Dalem Gedé Kusamba's artists created a vocabulary of movement for the monkey characters based on existing movements drawn from the various Sang Hyang genres. The mask of the Monkey King Sugriwa is considered to be the oldest and most sacred of the Kamasan masks; this is also the most sacred mask in the Barong Kedingkling group in Madangan. The vocabulary of movement employed by Sugriwa is the basis for the movement of all the monkeys. Unlike the simple realistic mimicry of monkey movements seen in Barong Kedingkling, in Wayang Wong the hopping, jumping, scratching and looking-around movements are stylized and choreographed—they have been transformed from pantomime into dance.

As the monkeys dance, they shout and squawk in a deafening chorus. Each monkey has an individual, characteristic, way of doing the basic pattern. The goat/monkey, Arimenda, gallops and butts with his horns; Sempati, the tiger/monkey, creeps and pounces; Satabali is a bird/monkey with chicken-like movements very similar to the movements of the kiuh/keker section of the Berutuk rite. These movements came into Wayang Wong from the old Balinese tradition but underwent a stylization and formalization when adapted for the Wayang Wong by the court artists of the eighteenth century.

Another important source for the Wayang Wong was Gambuh. The refined human characters—Rama, Sita, Laksmana, and Wibisana—are drawn directly from prototypes in the older form. The demonic characters Rawana, Kumbakarna, Indrajit, Prahasta, and Sukasrana wear dark red masks similar in style to those of the monkeys; these ogres all have prominent fangs. The vocabulary of movement they employ is taken from the strong characters of Gambuh. The costumes worn by the human characters and by the ogres are identical to the costumes worn in Gambuh, while the monkeys wear costumes like those of Baris, except that each is fitted with a long and prominent tail.

The source drawn on by the composers of Wayang Wong which gives the genre its name was Wayang Kulit, the shadow-puppet theatre.[8] Wayang, like Gambuh, came to Bali from Java, possibly as early as the ninth century A.D. and was associated with the Hindu culture of the Javanese courts and palaces. This form of theatre became very popular on Bali and remains so today; it is still practised by more than 300 *dalang*, or pup-

[68]

peteers. From the shadow-puppet theatre the makers of Wayang Wong received a prototype for the dramatization of material from the oldest group of literary-scriptural epics.

The *Ramayana* itself was a subject for representation in the shadow-theatre. Relief carvings dating from the fourteenth century exist at the Candi Panataran near Blitar in East Java in which episodes from the *Ramayana* are depicted.[9] The servant characters of the shadow-theatre are included in the panels, although they do not appear in the old *Ramayana* poem itself, indicating that the story was performed in the Wayang theatre of that time and that the sculptor drew inspiration from it in presenting the *Ramayana* tale in low relief. Some of the characters in the modern set of Balinese Wayang puppets are nearly identical to the figures depicted in the Panataran reliefs. The resemblance extends to the appearance of the monkey and servant characters in Wayang Wong, whose masks and headdresses definitely show the influence of the old East Javanese style. Other characters of the Panataran group, especially the ogres, like Kumbakarna, bear no particular likeness to modern Balinese shadow-puppets or to the masks of the demonic characters in Wayang Wong.

The shadow-theatre provided a great deal to the Wayang Wong. Certain aspects of the dancing—particularly the hand gestures—specifically imitate the movements of the shadow-puppets on the lighted screen. The music for Wayang Wong also came from the puppet-theatre; accompaniment is provided by the gamelan batel, an ensemble consisting of percussion instruments used in the gamelan gambuh plus the *gender wayang* ensemble, a quartet of metallophones played to accompany the shadow-play.

The percussion element brought to Wayang Wong the possibility for sophisticated co-ordination of dancers with the orchestra, under the guidance of the lead drummer and the cymbal player. The gender wayang ensemble made available the repertoire of theatrical music from the Wayang Kulit. The vocal music, which is sung exclusively by the dalang in the shadow-theatre, is apportioned among the dancers in Wayang Wong; as in most Balinese ensembles a lead singer in the gamelan batel provides a continuing vocal line.

The makers of Wayang Wong found a repertoire ready to hand in the plays of the dalang who performed the Wayang Kulit *Ramayana*, although the stories had to be simplified and adapted to suit the needs of the dramatic-dance medium. Dialogue in Wayang Wong is much simpler than in Wayang Kulit and there is less of it. Correspondingly, the proportion of the performance given over to dancing has been enlarged through the incorporation of *igel ngugal* (abstract introductory dances) adapted from those used in Gambuh.

The typical Wayang Wong performance is devoted to a single episode from the *Ramayana*; only in Pujungan Kaler, Gianyar Province, is there an attempted cutting of the entire long epic. In most villages the choice of story depends on the masks available. The story element is secondary in the standard performance of the present-day. The narrative serves mainly as a convenient framework for the succession of dances.

In Tejakula, Buleleng Province, the most complete set of Wayang Wong masks has been preserved. The collection includes two examples each of the masks for the four human characters, five principal ogres, a dozen principal monkeys, and twenty-four each of the ordinary unnamed monkeys and ogres. There are also four penasar. The masks in Tejakula belong to the Pasek Dangka clan; according to the four oldest dancers, men now in their eighties, the masks were a gift to the clan in the eighteenth century from the Raja of Bangli.

In Tejakula two particular old tales from the *Ramayana* have been preserved and are presented with as much fidelity to tradition as the four oldest dancers have been able to ensure. The two stories are done on consecutive days: 'The Death of Prahasta' is done on the first day, and 'The Death of Kumbakarna' is done on the second. The occasion for the performance is an Odalan at the principal temple of the clan; this always occurs at the same time as the most-important all-Balinese holiday *Galungan*, every 210 days. Participation is limited to members of the 150 families who make up the clan.

The Tejakula performances take place in the jaba tengah, or second temple courtyard, as in Gambuh. A very large kalangan is set up, and over it a temporary ceiling made of fresh greenery, flowers, and fruit is suspended. As in Gambuh the principal entrance is from the jeroan through a low archway. The gamelan and resting mats for waiting dancers are placed at the kelod end of the enclosure.

In the morning of the first of the two performance days, the dancers who will take part gather at the temple to receive their masks and gelung. More than fifty men participate. The group consists for the most part of dancers with very little training, except for the four old 'masters' who are in charge.[10] Nor is there a great deal of rehearsal. Participation in the performance is considered a form of devotional service to the temple. The older performers are trained dalang and dancers, and they dance the most difficult roles: Rama, Kumbakarna, Rawana, and Sugriwa. These roles also entail wearing the magically-powerful masks, and therefore men of great spiritual strength and learning are required to dance them. But the rest of the roles are danced by ordinary farmers and simple craftsmen.

The dancers receive their masks and head-dresses at the temple after a traditional rite for opening the niche in which these are stored between uses. Offerings are presented, and the masks are sprinkled with holy water before they are distributed. Then the dancers retire to make ready for the performance. Some of them go home to change, while others—who have come from great distances to take part—make their simple preparations nearby, outside the temple.

During this time it is customary for the dancers to hang their masks and gelung from the limbs of convenient tangerine and orange trees. Tejakula, located high on the mountain slopes, is well-known for its citrus fruit, which provides the village with an important source of income. Throughout the village the masks and gelung hang in the trees like artificial fruit. Just as in Barong Kedingkling, the Tejakula masks have a special association with productive trees and perhaps a special protective role to play on their behalf. The dancers decorate their head-dresses

[71]

with fresh leaves and flowers for the event.

On both days the performance begins in the early afternoon. A common pattern is followed. The play begins with a sequence of meeting scenes. On the first day Rama and his companions meet with the monkey leaders and their army in the first section; then Rawana meets with his ministers and the army of ogres. On the second day the sequence is reversed. These scenes have very little literary content. The dialogue is almost entirely made up of formal courtesies, and the movement of the action is interrupted time and again by extended igel ngugal, as character after character is presented, each with his own vocabulary of movement. The audience already knows the general line of the story, and the characters on stage do not need to present a detailed exposition of the action.

The four penasar characters are very prominent and active in Wayang Wong.[11] They are proportionately much more important than their equivalents in Gambuh. Twalen and Wredah, the attendants of the good party, have their counterparts in Delem and Sangut, who attend the ogres. These four characters are great favourites in Bali, where they are well-known from the Wayang Kulit. They serve similar functions as Togog and Semar: they translate from Kawi to Balinese; they elaborate and expand on the words of their masters, interpreting the meaning of the events of the story to the populace; and they take many opportunities to joke and clown.

In addition to their East Javanese ancestry they have a native background as well. 'Wredah' and 'Twalen' mean 'the old one' and 'the other old one' respectively in Balinese. The puppets representing these characters in Wayang Kulit have special ritual functions and are considered to be sacred characters, gods in disguise, even though they are often very earthy clowns. In Tunjuk, Tabanan Province, Twalen is the most sacred mask in the set of Wayang Wong masks kept by the Pasek Bendesa clan.

In the Wayang Wong performance the penasar come on stage before their masters appear. They explain the general situation in the course of their dialogue. The comic element is not extensively developed in the typical Wayang Wong perform-

[72]

ance, unlike Topeng Pajegan. The large masks worn by the penasar cover the dancers' faces and impede speech. The dancers struggle to project as well as they can, but in the comic realm simple physical comedy is the principal resource; Balinese audiences are very appreciative of slapstick humour. The four penasar serve as on-stage directors during the performance, making sure that the play moves along toward its conclusion.

The final section of the play is invariably devoted to fighting. First the ogres and monkeys struggle against one another in groups, and then the principals fight. Between the serious battles are comic interludes among the penasar. At the end Rawana's representative is always overcome, bringing the performance to a quick conclusion. The principal evil character, Rawana himself, is never killed.

In Tejakula the two performances are treated quite differently by the public, although the production is almost identical on each day. The first performance is always given on the day before the Odalan is to begin. It is regarded as a means of purifying the temple space and summoning the deities. Human spectators are irrelevant, for as a purely bebali performance it is addressed to the gods. Few people watch the performance, for most of the members of the clan are busily engaged with the completion of the preparations for the festival: chopping meat, making offerings, cooking, or perhaps joining the expedition up into the mountains for the purpose of fetching holy water at a sacred spring. Only children and those who are temporarily free from other responsibilities watch the dancers.

The second day's performance is received much differently, and all members of the clan as well as invited guests and other visitors join the audience. The only difference of any importance from the previous day is that the first meeting scene is extended by perhaps half an hour to include an edifying discourse on the nature of patriotism and good government, in Kawi, quoted directly from the *Ramayana*. Delem and Sangut translate and explain for the benefit of those spectators close enough to hear them. On this day the crowd is very attentive and rather grave in demeanour; a feeling of dignity is the dominant mood. All present are on their best behaviour to honour the distinguished guests, both human and divine.[12]

1. Goris (1954), I, p. 55; II, p. 121.

2. Even these accounts give little descriptive information.

3. Kakul (1979). See Emigh (1979) for a descriptive account of the performance and very interesting analysis of Topeng Pajegan.

4. Noosten (1936).

5. A copy of this manuscript is on deposit at Listibya Library, Denpasar.

6. Robson (1972).

7. Gralapp (1967).

8. deBoer (1979a).

9. Bernet-Kempers (1959).

10. deBoer (1979b) gives an account of a typical rehearsal of this type, conducted by another Balinese 'director', I Nyoman Rajeg, of Tunjuk village, Tabanan Province.

11. McPhee (1936, rep. 1970), pp. 154—5, describes these characters in detail.

12. Bandem (1980) is a comprehensive work on Wayang Wong.

4 Secular Dances in the Outer Temple

THE dance forms considered in this chapter are assigned to the *bali-balihan* group, which is made up of genres that are essentially secular in nature, presented purely for the entertainment of the audience. Performances of these forms can acquire a religious significance when they are given as part of a temple festival; then they are a contribution to the morale of the congregation, and the dancers are doing a kind of devotional service. But the same dances may also be performed for purely secular purposes, on purely secular occasions, and in purely secular spaces. Often the secular dances are given on a professional basis to raise money for the performing group through the sale of tickets.

The major genres in this category all descend directly from the three bebali forms. In all of them emphasis is primarily on aesthetic and entertainment values rather than on ritual or ceremonial dimensions. Natural talent and lengthy training are required of the performers, while audience participation is unimportant. It is perhaps too early to assess the most recent form, *Sendratari*, but the others may be assigned with confidence to the highest ranks of classical Balinese artistic achievement. All were created by sophisticated professional artists.

When secular dances are presented at an Odalan the temporary stage is set up in the third temple courtyard, called the *jaba* (literally, 'outside'), which is at once the least sacred and physically lowest part of the temple. During an Odalan the jaba is often crowded with people who are not busy at the time with formal activities or responsibilities. Although several necessary lesser rituals are performed in this space, it functions primarily as an area for entertainment and relaxation for members of the temple congregation.

The festival may occasionally continue for as long as ten days, and in many temples a dormitory is built in the jaba so that members from distant places will have lodging. Commerce is permitted in the jaba, and during the festival snacks, drinks and cigarettes are sold by women at small stands. Gamblers play cards and other games of chance. Often several gamelan groups

[75]

set up in the area and may play at the same time. The mood is noisy, relaxed, good-natured, active. Dance performances contribute to the festive atmosphere.

Legong

Of all the classical Balinese dances Legong is perhaps most familiar to Western audiences. Delicate, refined, and very intricate, the dance is performed by two or three pre-adolescent girls. The little dancers wear distinctive head-dresses and costumes as they perform a highly abstract dance-drama to the accompaniment of an old and sweet-sounding musical ensemble, the *gamelan pelegongan*. Dance lovers in many countries have come to appreciate the beauty of Legong after seeing performances given by touring dance groups or in film.

Legong is the oldest of the bali-balihan dances. An interesting account of its origin, which must have occurred around the turn of the nineteenth century, is given in the *Babad Dalem Sukawati*, a genealogical chronicle of the Princes of Sukawati. This village in Gianyar Province has long been famed for its excellence in the performing arts. According to the story, Legong was created as the result of a vision that came to the ruling Prince, I Dewa Agung Madé Karna, who was renowned for his spiritual powers. Once when he was meditating at the Pura Yogan Agung (Temple of the Great Meditation) in Ketewel village, near Sukawati, I Dewa Agung Madé Karna dreamt that he saw celestial maidens performing a dance in heaven; they were in the form of the young girls who dance while in a trance in the Sang Hyang Dedari, but they were dressed in colourful costumes rather than in white and wore golden head-dresses rather than the simple head-cloth. When he awoke the King called for the headman of Ketewel village and asked him to make some masks and to create a new dance resembling what he had seen in the dream.

Nine sacred masks were carved and painted by an artisan of the village, representing the nine celestial maidens of Hindu mythology. Two young Sang Hyang dancers were enlisted to perform with the masks and were taught a new dance composed for the occasion. These masks are still kept at the Pura Yogan Agung, where the old dance is performed every six months. The choreography seen in Sang Hyang Legong, as it is called, is quite simple but the form contains all the basic movements found in classical Legong dancing. Sang Hyang Legong is considered a wali dance, and it is performed in the jeroan.

Some time later a group directed by I Gusti Ngurah Jelantik (of the Jelantik family of Blahbatuh) created a new dance in a style similar to Sang Hyang Legong. In this new form, called *Nandir*, the dancers were young boys and masks were not used. Nandir was seen by the King of Gianyar, who was so much impressed by it that he commissioned a pair of artists from Sukawati to choreograph a similar dance for young girls of his court. The result of their efforts was the basis for Legong as we know it today. Unfortunately Nandir itself has passed out of existence. More classic than Legong and by all accounts very beautiful, the old form went into extinction for ever with the death of I Wayan Rindi, of Denpasar, who died in 1976. Pak Rindi was trained as a young Nandir dancer in Blahbatuh and was well-known for many years as a Legong teacher.

The creators of Legong worked with both wali and bebali elements in developing the new form. The basic musical and choreographic structures derive from Gambuh, while the source of the vocabulary of movement can be found in the Sang Hyang Dedari tradition. In Legong the pure dance passages serving to introduce important characters in the bebali genres (igel ngugal) have been expanded and developed. The narrative element, although still present in skeletal form, has been de-emphasized. The result is well along in the direction toward a pure dance composition.

The choreography of the Legong performance follows the structure of the music, which was adapted from the accompaniment to Gambuh. The long first part of the presentation, which is the same no matter what story is presented, is accompanied by a composition in three parts: *pengawit* (head), *pengawak* (body), and *pengecet* (tail). In the pengawit the three little dancers are introduced. One of them, dressed slightly different from the other two, comes first. She is the *Condong*, or maidservant to the others. She dances at length with two fans which she will present to her mistresses when they enter. She dances for perhaps ten minutes in a complicated and difficult solo which covers the entire stage and demonstrates the full vocabulary of the beautiful Legong style. She greets her diminutive mistresses courteously, bending low in their presence, and presents them with their fans before taking her departure.

Now the pengawak begins. This section is very elegant and is somewhat slower than the pengawit; in the complete classical performance it is perhaps twenty minutes long. The two dancers move in unison through a symmetrical choreographic pattern in close co-ordination with the drumming and cymbals. The final section, the pengecet, begins as the gamelan doubles the tempo. The dancers face each other and dance vigorously, yet precisely; they mirror each other, flicking quick glances of the eyes and jerking their heads from side to side. Their fans are in active motion, almost drawing a design in the air. The tempo accelerates and then suddenly comes to an abrupt halt.

Now the dramatic section of the performance begins. The lead singer has sung texts from the old Kawi poem Malat during the first section of the performance. Now he serves as narrator, and recites the background to the play in high Balinese from his place in the orchestra, against a background of soft instrumental music in a melancholy mode. In the most commonly presented story, 'Lasem', the situation described concerns a meeting between the King of Lasem and Princess Rangke Sari, whom he has kidnapped. She does not love him and prefers her betrothed, Prince Panji Inu Kertapati.

The little dancers appear, and the scene becomes a pengipuk, or courtship dance. The two characters are identical in appearance and style of movement—in Legong there is no differentiation of the characters according to type, and all of the movement belongs to the refined category. After rejecting Lasem's advances the Princess tells him that she will only marry him if he can defeat Prince Panji in battle. Dialogue and description are provided by the singer, for although the dancers are not masked they never speak or sing.

The pangkat or departure—similar to the departure of Panji's group in Gambuh—occurs next. This section is sometimes extended to include mimed riding on horseback as the unlucky King makes his way toward the battlefield. Either he dances alone or he is accompanied by the second dancer as he travels. Suddenly the Condong reappears with stylized wings of carved and gilded leather clasped to her forearms; she represents now a bird of ill omen, Guwak, the crow. This is a form of *pesiat*, or fight scene. At the end Lasem drives off the crow before he exits to face what everyone knows will be certain death at the hands of Prince Panji. The two dancers return to the stage to dance a short abstract epilogue (*pekaad*) which brings the performance to an end.

Other stories can be told in Legong, with suitable adaptation of the basic structure of stock scenes. In Benoh village, Badung Province, for example, a story from the *Ramayana* involving the fight of the two rival monkeys, Subali and Sugriwa, is a favourite. Again no masks are worn, and the characters are difficult to tell apart. The member of the audience who does not understand Balinese may find it difficult to keep track of the particulars of the story. As many as fifteen different stories were adapted to the Legong in the nineteenth century, but most of them have fallen out of use in recent times. Today more than ever, Legong owes its popularity to excellence in dancing rather than to the narrative element.

Like other court arts of pre-colonial Bali, Legong served in the traditional palace as an expression and display of the wealth, power, and glory of the ruling Prince. The realm was searched for its most beautiful and talented little girls, many of whom became royal wives and concubines. The dancers were dressed in expensive costumes decorated with gold leaf and costly jewels. They received a lengthy professional training. No village or minor family could at first afford the expense of maintaining these ornaments for the royalty. But in contrast to the court dancers of Java, the Legong dancers of Bali were not often themselves of high-caste origin.

Already in the mid-nineteenth century there was a movement of trained Legong dancers from the palaces back to the villages, as girls who had been trained at court returned to their birth-places or went to other villages. Some of them had already served as teachers at court. With the encouragement of lesser gentry in towns at some distance from the great palaces, clubs were established to perform the popular dance at the local level. The village group might receive a subsidy and encouragement from the sponsor but it was free to perform at Odalan in the village temple, and even outside the village, for a fee. This was exactly the case at the village of Saba, Gianyar Province, which has been a centre for training teachers and performers of Legong since the early nineteenth century.

Other villages such as Sukawati, Bedulu, and Peliatan became known for Legong as well, and many students from all over Bali were sent to learn the dance in the schools set up in these cultural centres in Gianyar Province. By the time of the Dutch colonial take-over of Bali, Legong had spread to many of the larger villages and towns and had become in many places a truly popular art form, maintained by and for the village communities. It was and still is performed as entertainment in connection with temple festivals in many villages. Communities that do not themselves have a Legong group might hire a club from one of the famous villages, or might work out an exchange arrangement, performing their Wayang Wong, for example, in return for the borrowed services.

Kebyar

After the Dutch completed their take-over of Bali in 1908, Buleleng Province in North Bali grew in importance, for the capital city Singaraja became the seat of the Dutch colonial administration. The culture of North Bali had previously been somewhat cut off from the south, for passage is difficult across the great central mountain range, and the border states were often at war. A great cultural renaissance began in North Bali in the early years of the twentieth century. Many new gamelan and dance clubs were founded and creative activity flourished. Among the forms newly created or reinvigorated was one which was to take all Bali by storm, *Kebyar*. Its source was Legong, but its inspiration was competitive pride.

We have mentioned earlier that it is common at an Odalan for two or even more gamelan to set up and play in the jaba area of the temple at the same time. Under some circumstances this can become a kind of 'battle of the bands', in which two instrumental groups compete to see which can attract the greatest number of spectators and the loudest support. In the early years of this century two villages in North Bali, Jagaraga and Bungkulan, had an especially intense rivalry and competed on a regular basis in creating new music and dance compositions. Bungkulan contributed a new musical idea in which a virtuoso performer would alternately sing and play the *trompong*, an old-fashioned musical instrument consisting of a row of knobbed gongs in a carved wooden case. He was accompanied by the full gamelan.

In 1914, Jagaraga contributed the *Kebyar Legong*, a dance performed by two young women dressed in men's clothing, who interpreted the music of the accompanying orchestra in a pure dance medium. There was no plot, but the dancers presented a kind of character study of a young man. Modern Kebyar grew out of a combination of the ideas proposed by the two groups, although Jagaraga has received most of the credit for the new development. The new musical ideas in particular swept quickly over the entire island of Bali. Kebyar ('lightning') style is florid, complex, dynamic, and highly embellished. Compared to the traditional gamelan music it sounds almost supercharged.

By 1919 the style was well established. The King of Tabanan, who served also as the Dutch regent for his province, sent for a Kebyar orchestra (from North Bali) in that year to play at an important cremation. In the audience was a young and very talented dancer, I Nyoman Mario, who was much impressed by

[81]

what he heard and who undertook to develop further the possibilities for dance in the new style. His great contribution to Balinese culture was ready in 1925 when he presented *Kebyar Duduk* for the first time.

From Bungkulan Mario took the idea of playing the trompong in virtuoso manner during the performance. This old instrument had fallen out of favour among Balinese musicians, but Mario restored it to a starring role in the ensemble. He developed a flashy style of playing the instrument, with whirling sticks and flourishing gestures. He had to squat behind the instrument to be able to play it, and this suggested that the entire composition might be performed in a sitting (*duduk*) position. He took the costume from Kebyar Legong, but to move in a squatting position he had to hold up the train with one hand as he moved. This became a hallmark of the new genre.

The mood of Kebyar Duduk is determined by the music, and the dancer works in close co-ordination with the entire gamelan to interpret its shifting colours. Many of the basic poses, gestures, and longer phrases of movement have been adapted from Legong, but they have been made more intricate, more elaborate, and more artificial. In Kebyar Duduk there is no pantomime whatever, and the narrative element is absent. The Legong dancer works in close relationship with the patterns set by the drummers in the gamelan, but in Kebyar the entire ensemble of twenty-five to thirty musicians starts and stops in sudden cadences (*angsel*) when the dancer comes to an abrupt, accented pause.

The dance is set to a single musical composition which lasts for perhaps twenty minutes. It is above all a form for the young dancer, as the demands on the performer's legs are very exacting. The piece progresses through a sequence of moods of an idealized Balinese youth who is just at the point of reaching full maturity. He expresses a gamut of emotions, ranging from sweet flirtatiousness to bashfulness, melancholy and angry bravado. In a sense the entire study is a refined distillation of the manifold qualities demonstrated by the young men of Trunyan in the Berutuk rite. No solo in Balinese dance is more demanding in terms of technique and sheer physical strength than Kebyar Duduk.

The Kebyar style of music and the new dance by Mario swept over the entire island of Bali with a swiftness that seemed to mark it as a craze or fad, and possibly a short-lived one. Other genres of dance and drama, such as *Stambul*, *Drama Gong*, and to some extent *Janger*, became very popular in Bali for a brief time before fading quickly. But the Kebyar enthusiasm has already been strong for more than fifty years and shows no sign of weakening. Kebyar has become *the* established Balinese style of dance and music; its influence can be felt in every corner of the Balinese performing arts.

A great deal of new dance composition has been done in Bali since Mario first created Kebyar Duduk, and with few exceptions, Kebyar has been the dominant style visible in the new work. The still-popular *Panji Semirang*, for example, was composed in 1933 by the great Legong teacher, I Nyoman Kaler, of Kelandis village, Badung Province. This piece was composed to answer the need for a composition in Kebyar style suitable for a female dancer; it had been learnt earlier on that women could do the movements required in Kebyar Duduk but had trouble capturing the appropriate moods. In Panji Semirang the dancer portrays Princess Candra Kirana, well known from the Malat poem as well as from Gambuh.

The princess—in disguise as a young man—is portrayed at a time when she is searching through the world for her lover, Panji. She visits the court of a foreign kingdom and there performs a dance for the assembled courtiers; as she dances she searches the crowd with her eyes to see if her lover is present. The dance itself is similar to Kebyar Duduk in form and style. The dancer portrays a shifting sequence of moods, as she searches in vain for Panji, and then exults to see him in the audience. The short piece concludes on a joyful note. This composition also met with popular success all over Bali, and thereafter Kebyar dance came to be known popularly as *Kebyar Bebancihan* (Neutered Kebyar), or even plain 'Bebancihan' (neuter), because it was no longer restricted to male performers.

Between 1925 and the early 1950s Balinese choreographers created a number of new dances for women in Kebyar style. Kebyar Duduk, which was performed brilliantly by Mario himself and later by a series of his students, remained popular for male dancers. Some of the many new compositions for women were *Mergapati* ('King of the Lions'), *Wiranata* ('Brave King'), and *Yudapati* ('King of Battle'). In all of them female soloists presented male character studies similar to those of Kebyar Duduk. These forms survive today. In none of them is the difficult squat-walk of Kebyar Duduk to be found, but in style they are pure Kebyar.

In 1931 the first full group of Balinese dancers and musicians performed in Europe, presenting a series of concerts at the Colonial Exhibition in Paris. A group from Ubud, Gianyar Province, led by Cokorda Gedé Sukawati, danced for wildly enthusiastic audiences which included the great French director and dramatic theorist, Antonin Artaud.[1] Legong and Kebyar Duduk were on the programme. Another important tour to Europe and America was organized in 1953, soon after Indonesia had become independent.[2] This tour was organized by an American, John Coast, with Mario, and the Anak Agung Gedé Mandra, Prince of Peliatan, who was master, teacher and leader of the group.

When the performance was being assembled it became apparent to the leaders that there was a shortage of material suitable for presentation to Western audiences; because of language and cultural barriers, many of the Balinese dramatic dance genres were felt to be unsuitable. Accordingly, Mario was asked to create a new dance for the tour in Kebyar style. His creation, called *Tumulilingan* ('Bumble-bees'), is a pengipuk (courtship dance) for two performers, male and female. They represent in abstract fashion two bumble-bees which are playing in a garden. Accessibility for foreign audiences was already a factor in the development of Balinese dance by this time, but the new form was accepted with enthusiasm by Balinese audiences and dancers at the end of the tour, and the duet has established a secure place in the Balinese repertoire.

[84]

Thus it is given quite often in connection with temple festivals; like all the bali-balihan genres it acquires religious significance in that context.

Tari Tani

In the early years of Indonesian independence the new national government and a number of the then-emerging political parties actively supported the development of new forms of dance, partly in an effort to make use of the popular arts to gain support for political causes. These efforts resulted in the creation of a number of new genres in Bali, in the Kebyar style of dancing, but based on pantomime and patriotic thematic material. The pantomimic gestures were developed from observed activities of everyday life among the common people. One such creation was the *Tari Tani* ('Peasant Dance'), sponsored by the Nationalist Party (*PNI*), and choreographed by a group of artists in Kerambitan, Tabanan Province. In this piece seven dancers, six women and a man, enact in pantomime the sequence of tasks involved in planting, cultivating, and harvesting rice. Other dances sponsored by other groups portrayed the daily tasks of fishermen and of coffee plantation workers; in his seventieth year Pak Kaler of Kelandis even attempted to create a dance of this type based on the movements of a badminton player. None of these dances makes use of speech, although some of them end with choral singing in Balinese on the benefits of mutual aid and co-operation.

The vocabulary of movement employed in these programmatic dances is entirely new and quite realistic. It grew out of the direct observation of nature. Perhaps for the first time in hundreds of years Balinese choreographers turned away from the worked and reworked materials passed down in their traditional heritage. The dances, however, are firmly set to the musical accompaniment provided by the *gamelan gong kebyar*, newest and most brilliant (and perhaps loudest) of the orchestral ensembles of Bali. In good Kebyar style the compositions feature very complicated patterns of rhythmic accents and quick angsel (cadences) in which the gamelan and the dancers come to a sudden, simultaneous, pause.

Kebyar style here is overlaid on movement quite foreign to the traditional Balinese dance vocabulary and it can therefore be seen for what it is: a mode of embellishment growing out of a set of rhythmic ideas. The basic pattern might be spoken as 'Tut cheng cheng tut cheng!' Like flamboyant art all over the world, Kebyar's highly ornamented surfaces are best supported by relatively simple structures.

Sendratari

In 1962 a team of Balinese artists connected with the government high school for the performing arts (KOKAR) created a new dance composition, in which the Kebyar style was employed for the presentation of a lengthy dance-drama. The story was the popular Balinese favourite *Jayaprana*, told in its entirety by a large company of student dancers, through gesture and pan-tomime. No words were necessary for the meaning to be understood, although educated Balinese could follow the narrative in Kawi and Balinese provided by the *juru tandak* from his place in the gamelan. The movement used by the dancers was entirely pantomime ornamented with decorative Kebyar embellishments. The new form was called *Sendratari* (modern dance-drama) *Jayaprana*. Audiences were very enthusiastic, both at the school where it was first performed, and later in villages all over Bali.

In 1965 the KOKAR group produced another dance-drama of the same type, based on the *Ramayana*, which met with even greater success. Soon many villages had established *Sendratari Ramayana* groups of their own to perform as bali-balihan, whether in connection with their own village Odalan, or for hire to other villages, or for tourist audiences at hotels and else-where. The original creators of the genre were much influenced by the success of the Javanese *Ramayana Ballet*, first shown at Prambanan in Central Java in 1961. That performance had been established with government support to provide a cultural entertainment which could be understood by foreigners as well as by Indonesians from all over the Republic. Balinese Sendratari was devised to meet the same needs.

By 1978 seven different classics of Balinese traditional literature had been adapted for presentation in the Sendratari mode by faculty members at KOKAR, working under the artistic leadership of I Wayan Brata, a well-known choreographer and composer. Village performances of *Ramayana*, wherever they are given in Bali, are based firmly on the prototype presented at KOKAR. Indeed, all of the teachers who have brought the genre into the villages have been alumni of the school. Just as the court culture of the Hindu-Balinese rulers of the eighteenth and nineteenth centuries served as a force in the direction of standardization in Balinese culture, government-sponsored schools, research teams, and creative projects now tend to exert a unifying influence across the island.

The Sendratari performances have all been conceived for an 'end stage', similar to a Western proscenium stage, which is the form of the theatre on the KOKAR campus. In the villages substitute arrangements have had to be made. Most often the performance is given in the *balé banjar* (town hall), or in a cockfighting arena in the jaba area of the temple. This disposition of the stage space has led to the use of many Western principles of stage composition, at the expense perhaps of some of the intimacy of a performance given in the three-sided kalangan.

As in the programmatic dances, in *Ramayana* the Kebyar style of ornamentation is applied over a simple foundation of pantomimic story-telling. Even young children can follow the narrative. But at the same time, the difficult accents and flourishes of the Kebyar style provide interest and pleasure for the connoisseur of pure dance. The musical structure brings together compositions from several different Balinese dance traditions in a clever two-hour anthology unified by its stylistic treatment. In good Balinese tradition the play includes a comic fight sequence, involving Anoman and two ogres; these performers need acrobatic skills as well. When possible the play is lighted with Western electrical equipment. The colourful costumes are a modern creation, based on traditional Balinese costumes but fitted with head-dresses adapted from the shadow-puppet theatre.

With Sendratari we near the end of our discussion of dances which have emerged thus far in the Kebyar style. We have seen that Kebyar developed from Legong and that it gave rise to many forms of modern composition. It should also be noticed that Kebyar's influence also extended backward, affecting its source. In 1932 Ida Bagus Boda, of Kaliungu, Badung Province, re-choreographed the pengawit section of the Legong in a style heavily influenced by Kebyar. Subsequently the body of the dance was also elaborated, and a more difficult pattern of angsel was introduced. These changes were adopted quickly everywhere.

Legong itself has influenced its own sources. The Sang Hyang Dedari dancers of Bona village, Gianyar Province, now dress in the complete Legong costume with its golden aprons and head-dresses rather than in their traditional simple white cloth costume. At the conclusion of their 'tour' in trance around the village, the little dancers of Bona stop outside the temple and give a complete Legong performance. The pattern of interrelations among the genres becomes ever more complex with time, because new creation in Bali, especially in Balinese music and dance, arises very often from the transposition of the materials from one genre into the medium of another.

Parwa

There is a story in Sukawati village that tells the origin of *Parwa*; it may indeed be true. During most of the nineteenth century the Kings of Gianyar were at odds or worse with their nominal superiors, the Kings of Klungkung. Finally in 1885 the King of Klungkung was able to capture the King of Gianyar by trickery, and at that time many members of Gianyar's royal household were sent into exile to desolate Nusa Penida, a small and inhospitable island off the Balinese coast.

Many dancers and musicians were in the group, and to pass

the time they decided to present a performance. Although they had no masks or costumes at hand, they were able to devise a new kind of dramatic dance very similar in many ways to Wayang Wong. Realizing however that it would be impossible to portray the monkeys and ogres of the *Ramayana* repertoire without special equipment, the artists-in-exile looked to the *Mahabharata* for source material. Luckily a dalang was among them, and with his help an unmasked dance-drama was created. The tradition was continued after the courtiers were rescued from Nusa Penida and allowed to return home. For years Sukawati was famous for its Parwa, but the group disbanded in 1967, when the great Sukawati dalang, I Nyoman Granyam, leader, teacher and organizer of the group, passed away.

In the Parwa performance, the characters alternate speech with singing; nearly equal weight is given to each mode of expression. The musical repertoire comes from the Wayang Kulit, and the dialogue is also in the Wayang manner. Granyam's ward in the village of Sukawati, Banjar Babakan, has long been unusual in providing a home for as many as a dozen active professional dalang at a time; these expert actors and singers are absolutely fluent in Kawi and can even improvise freely in the ancient language.

Granyam's group rehearsed diligently and regularly under the master's own supervision, and even today the Sukawati Parwa group is remembered with respect for its high level of achievement and fidelity to tradition. The style of dance movement in Parwa shows strong and direct influence from Gambuh: Wayang Wong has an insufficient cast of human characters to provide prototypes for the five Pandawa heroes, their matronly mother, and the hundred evil Kurawas, and so the Demang and the Tumenggung, the Prabu, Prabangsa, Panji, the Putri, and the Condong all appear with names and in situations from the old Parwa (chapters) of the *Mahabharata*. The Putri's ladies-in-waiting, the kakan-kakan, also appear in Parwa, in a dance which shows strong influence of Legong style. Their dance is quick and energetic; they call to one another as they dance in unison. In Parwa as in Legong, the eye-flicking movements (*seledet*) and side-to-side jerks of the head (*engotan*) are very prominently featured.

At the present time only one group presenting Parwa is active in Bali. This organization, called the '*Seka Parwa Agung*' ('the Great Parwa Group'), is led by Ida Bagus Sarga, of Bongkasa village, Badung Province. Pak Sarga is Bali's best-known dalang performing the *Ramayana* repertoire, and he is an expert on many aspects of Balinese performing art. In the performance given by his group the penasar characters wear no masks, but employ modern make-up. The level of their performance is high, and they are called upon to perform fairly often at Odalan in the villages, and in the government Art Centre on public holidays such as Indonesia's Independence Day, 17 August.

Arja

In 1825 King I Dewa Agung Gedé Kusamba of Klungkung, highest in rank of the Balinese Princes, died at the end of a fifty-year reign. His cremation ceremony was one of the most magnificent in Balinese history. Lower-ranked monarchs from all the other Balinese kingdoms attended the ceremonies and contributed generously to the rites. Although the King had quarrelled incessantly with his nominally subordinate neighbours, the Kings of Badung and Gianyar dispatched court Gambuh dancers and musicians to help with preparations for the ceremony. The combined group created a special new performance for the cremation.

The innovation was called *Dadap* because two dadap trees, traditionally associated with funeral rites on the island, were planted at opposite ends of the kalangan.[3] The all-male company of dancers surprised and delighted the public by singing the dialogue of the play, as in Western opera. Dadap was a great success and thereafter performing groups were established in most of the court cities.

The new form came to be known as *Arja* and proved to be very popular among the general population; by the early twentieth century it had spread all over the island, sponsored by villages and kin-groups. Today Arja is Bali's most popular theatrical genre. Visitors to Bali find the form somewhat inaccessible because of language barriers.

In the Gambuh performance, emphasis is allotted more or less equally among three major elements: music, dance, and literary-theatrical features. In each of the nineteenth-century genres based on Gambuh, one or another of these components is emphasized at the expense of the others. In Legong and its derivatives, stress was placed on the purely 'dancerly' features of Gambuh, and narrative was de-emphasized or eliminated. Vocal music was taken from the dancer and assigned to a specialist in the gamelan.

In Arja by contrast the vocal music became paramount, especially after the 1920s when women replaced male performers in the four principal roles. The Kawi language was replaced by Balinese at the same time, yielding a more easily understandable popular medium. The introduction of female singers/dancers inspired a great new enthusiasm for Arja, for to the Balinese ear, women's voices are better suited to singing the *tembang* (songs).

Arja is technically very demanding. Not only must the performer sing beautifully, but she must be able to dance well at the same time. The melodic patterns sung are pre-established, but much of the content of the play is improvised during the performance. The singer must co-ordinate the phrasing of the vocal line with the phrasing of the gesture and fit both precisely to the accompaniment. Long training and great inherent talent are required. The very best performers soon became known outside their own localities and were sought for professional engagements with other groups. Early in this century a kind of indigenous 'star system' had come into existence.

Prior to the colonial period communications among the various regions of Bali were poor, owing to the constant wars among the small kingdoms and to difficult terrain. But after the Dutch constructed modern roads and bridges, and above all since radio station was established, it has been possible for some performers to acquire an island-wide reputation. In 1958 a regular Sunday Arja performance was begun on Radio Republik Indonesia, under the leadership of I Madé Kredek of Singapadu village, Gianyar Province. The programme has been very popular ever since; many people plan their week-end schedules around the broadcast. Arja is better adapted to radio dissemination than other forms, since the singing is almost continuous throughout the performance, and a member of the radio audience can follow the events exactly. Cassette tape recordings have also become widely available in recent years, and these have also tended to promote the reputations of the most popular and well-known performers.

Another point of emphasis in the Arja performance is humour and clowning. No fewer than eight penasar appear in the list of standard characters. Even the original Dadap production produced for the cremation of King I Dewa Agung Gedé Kusamba had an important satirical dimension. King Kusamba had had two wives, one a beautiful princess from Badung, the other a stout matron from Karangasem. The second wife was as strong-willed and powerful as she was unattractive, and many people hated her, especially in Badung. The story chosen for the Dadap performance at the cremation was *Kasayangan Limbur* ('Loves of the Ugly Queen'); in it the deceased King and his wife were discreetly satirized. The Limbur, who parodied the Queen from Karangasem, became a favourite type-character in Arja, along with her three comic attendants.

The refined hero figure in Arja, whatever his name may be in the particular story, is attended by two penasar who have become prototypical in many modern varieties of dance-drama. These characters are Punta and Kartala; they are unmasked counterparts to the *penasar kelihan* and *penasar cenikan* of Topeng Pajegan. Punta is the somewhat pompous and self-important straight man and butt for his more clever partner's jokes and pranks. The Condong (maidservant) is also prominently featured in Arja, and in the other modern dance-dramas.

[92]

Modern Baris

It is unclear when and where the first modern variations on the old Baris Gedé were introduced, but they seem to be an early twentieth-century development. As in Legong the wali tradition provided materials for the creation of a sophisticated new dance. The soloist wears the distinctive costume of Baris Gedé, with its shimmering pointed helmet. The basic movements have been taken from the older dance as well, but they have been refined and embellished to a considerable degree.

Like Kebyar, solo Baris presents a plotless character study. The personage is a traditional Balinese warrior, stronger and more mature than the somewhat effeminate taruna of Kebyar Duduk. The dance is said by some to represent abstractly the conduct of the warrior on the battlefield, as he manoeuvres to avoid attack. Certainly the character is tense—in fact he trembles with nervous excitement—and his eyes dart from side to side. There is no narrative in the fifteen-minute solo, which is accompanied by the gamelan gong. Solo Baris is commonly performed as part of a programme consisting of several different kinds of dance, such as Kebyar, Legong, Tumulilingan, etc.

The basic solo Baris dance has become in recent times the fundamental dance in the training of the male dance student. Professional dance teachers feel that Baris is ideal for the purpose in that the form is quite straightforward, yet it contains all the essential elements of classical Balinese dance as it is performed today. At ASTI, the government-sponsored college-level conservatory of dance and music, Baris is also included in the first-year curriculum of female dancers, although Legong is considered to be the fundamental female dance style.

Some time after the modern Baris appeared as a pure dance solo, it occurred to choreographers in Gianyar Province to create a story-telling dance form using the popular new character, just as the makers of Legong had done a century earlier. Thus the Baris Melampahan ('Story Baris') came into being. Plays based on stories from the *Mahabharata* and *Ramayana* have been especially popular subjects for representation by companies including one or more Baris dancers, complete with their uniform costume, in leading roles. Just as the Legong dancers do not alter their appearance to differentiate characters, the *baris* may represent someone refined or coarse—or even animal—without altering the vocabulary of the established style.

A Baris Melampahan performance is often preceded by a series of introductory solo Baris dances, like the introductory masks in the Topeng Pajegan. Two penasar, Punta and Kartala, always appear; they speak for their masters who, although unmasked, never speak or sing. The baris communicates in gesture alone. He may speak to Punta, for example, by gesturing at him while Kartala provides the sound, just as if he were dubbing a foreign film. The language spoken for the baris is Kawi. Then Punta will explain what has been said to him, in Balinese, so that the audience can understand.

Panyembrama

This recent purely secular composition was created in 1967 from the sacred Rejang dance by I Gusti Raka Saba, who was the Legong teacher at ASTI. It took its present form after some reworking by I Wayan Brata of KOKAR-Bali in 1970. The piece is a group work for five female dancers who carry bowls with flower petals and burning sticks of incense. It is in modern Kebyar style. Developed from rites to honour the visiting gods, the piece has been adapted to show honour to the guests in attendance at the performance. At the conclusion the young women strew flower petals toward the audience. The costume is an elaborate new creation based on the simpler Rejang costume.

Panyembrama ('Greeting') is always given as the first number in the concert programme. Recently the dance has come to be given as a matter of routine at Ngurah Rai Airport when distinguished guests from Jakarta or foreign dignitaries arrive. As many as thirty dancers may take part. Certain villages near the airport have organized groups who work on a money-making basis when hired by travel agents, hotels, or the government. In recent years, it has become common for women who have received dance training to perform Panyembrama in the context of a village Odalan, where once Mendet or Gabor might have been done. Here we see a movement from the secular toward the sacred, as a bali-balihan genre becomes a wali one.

Topeng Panca

At the end of the nineteenth century the King of Badung had assembled a truly superior group of dancers to perform at court. Some of the artists were of the brahmana caste while others were commoners. Ida Bagus Boda, who later conceived the modern choreography for the Condong in Legong, was leader of the group. Since there were five dancers who were all expert performers of Topeng, Ida Bagus Boda was inspired to assemble a performance in which the entire group could take part. This, unlike Topeng Pajegan, was to be an entirely secular perform-ance to be given for the entertainment of the ruler and his family. It was called Topeng Panca (Five-Man Topeng). The basic structure of Topeng Pajegan needed very little adaptation to serve the needs of the group, and the repertoire was taken from the same historical sources used in the earlier ritual Topeng. The innovation proved to be very popular, and after Badung fell to the Dutch in 1906 the company went 'on the road'. They per-formed in many of the larger settlements of the island and inspired many imitators. The genre is still very popular among Balinese audiences today.

The additional performers create new possibilities for humour by comparison with the old Topeng Pajegan, for two clowns have more scope than one. Bondres scenes are protracted in Topeng Panca, and the performance lasts much longer than the solo form does, to allow for extended clowning. Occasionally a Baris dancer now performs as part of the introductory group of masks. The action proceeds more smoothly than in ritual Topeng, since no pause is needed while the dancer is off-stage changing mask and head-dress. The Sidha Karya character does not appear.

[95]

Prembon

As the twentieth century progressed, more and more new combinations of previously separate dance genres have been made, yielding a bewildering variety of hybrid and composite forms. During the troubled 1940s, the last of the traditional line of the Kings of Gianyar, I Dewa Mangis VIII, called together the dancers attached to his palace and asked them to create *Prembon* ('Combination'). He asked that favourite type characters be taken from Gambuh, Baris, Arja, Topeng and Parwa, and that a single story be presented in which they all appeared. The clowns were taken from Topeng, while Baris provided the protagonist. The Princess and the Condong from Arja took the leading female roles, while Prabangsa from Gambuh appeared as the strong Patih. Once again the Topeng repertoire, dealing with the historical Kings of Bali, was the source of subject matter. Music for the performance was composed to be played on the gamelan gong.

This new mixture of traditional and modern elements has found favour with Balinese audiences, as well as with performers, especially in villages where there are dancers who are trained in different styles and genres. Prembon makes it possible for all to contribute to the Odalan in a single performance.

1. Artaud's (1958) evocative essay, written after seeing one of these performances, first brought the Balinese theatre to the attention of Western artists. 'In a word, the Balinese have realized, with the utmost rigor, the idea of pure theatre. . . .' The essay although misinformed in a number of particulars is correct in spirit.

2. Coast (1953) describes the story of this tour and its formation.

3. See above, pp. 20–1.

1 *Sang Hyang Dedari*, Bona. A dancer enters trance. *Kidung* singers at left, *Cak* group at right rear. (Courtesy Danielle Toth)

2 *Sang Hyang Dedari*, Bona. The dancers in a trance. (Courtesy Danielle Toth)

3 *Topeng*, Mask of Tua (old man).

4 *Topeng,* the Dalem (refined king).

5 *Topeng*, Mask of Bondesa
(village chief)

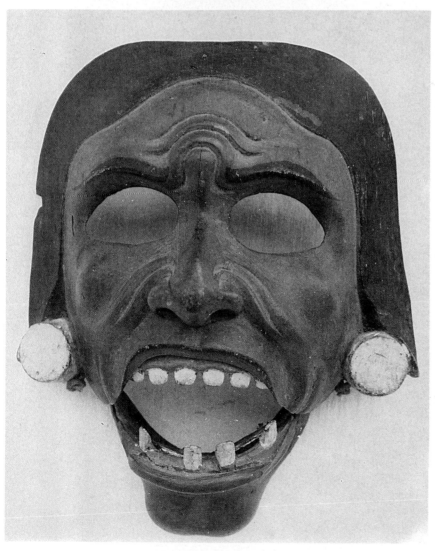

6 *Topeng*, Mask of female *bondres*
(comic villager).

7 *Topeng*, Mask of Putri (refined princess).

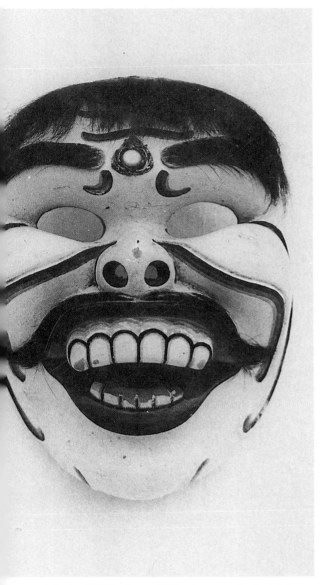

openg, Mask of Sidha Karya ('He who can do the job').

9 *Jauk*, Mask.

10 Bhima Swarga, Parwa story.

1 *Berutuk* rite, Trunyan.

2 *Berutuk* rite, Trunyan. The King.

3 *Berutuk* rite, Trunyan. The Patih.

4 *Rejang*, Bungaya, Karangasem.

5 *Rejang* procession, Tenganan.

6 '*Bayu, sabda, idep*': Balinese prayer.

7 *Baris Gedé*, Batur, Kintamani.

8 *Baris Gedé* (*Baris Poleng* variant), Sanur.

9 *Memendet*, Kebon Bukit, Karangasem.

10 *Gambuh*, Batuan, Putri and Condong (princess and maidservant). (Courtesy Danielle Toth)

11 *Gambuh*, Padang Aji, Karangasem. Old Patih (prime minister).

12 *Gambuh*, Batuan. Panji (refined hero). (Courtesy Danielle Toth)

13 *Gambuh*, Batuan. Panji scene, with *arya-arya* (courtiers)
and Semar (servant).

14 *Gambuh*, Batuan. Prabu (Antagonist King).

15 *Gambuh*, Batuan. The *gamelan*, with *gambuh* flutes.
(Courtesy Danielle Toth)

16 *Wayang Wong*, Mask of Wibisana.
(Courtesy Swasthi Bandem)

17 *Wayang Wong*, Mask of Kumbakarna. (Courtesy Swasthi Bandem)

18 *Wayang Wong*, Tunjuk, Tabanan. Sugriwa with his servants,
Twalen and Wredah.

19 *Wayang Wong*, Bangli. Anoman.

20 *Wayang Wong*, Tejakula, Buleleng. From left, Wibisana, Twalen, Laksmana.

21 *Wayang Wong*, Tunjuk. Masks of the four *penasar*: Twalen (black mask at left) is sacred, Wredah, Delem, Sangut.

22 *Legong*, Tabanan.

23 *Legong*, Peliatan, Gianyar. *Pengipuk* (courtship scene).

4 *Kebyar Duduk*, Peliatan. Dancer at the *trompong*.

25 *Tumulilingan*, Peliatan. The female dancer.

26 *Parwa*, Bongkasa, Badung. Arjuna.

27 *Arja*, Singapadu, Gianyar. The Condong, portrayed
by Ni Nyoman Candri.

28 *Arja*, Singapadu. Mantri Buduh (Antagonist King), attended by two *penasar* meets Galuh (Princess).

29 *Arja*, Singapadu. From left, Condong, Galuh, Mantri Manis (Protagonist King), Prince.

30 Solo *Baris*, Kelandis, Denpasar.

31 Solo *Baris*, Lebah.

32 *Panyembrama*, Peliatan.

33 *Topeng Panca*, Singapadu. Penasar Cenik
(younger servant).

34 *Topeng Panca*, Singapadu. Dalem and Penasar.

35 *Topeng Panca*, Singapadu. Penasar Cenik and *bondres* character.

36 *Barong Ket*. (Courtesy Swasthi Bandem)

37 *Barong Ket*, Banjar Boni, Kuta, Badung. In procession at the New Year.
(Courtesy Gen' ichi Tsuge)

38 *Rangda*.

39 *Onying* (self-stabbing).

40 *Calonarang* Dance-drama. Punta and Kartala (servants).

41 *Calonarang*, Pandung (The Prime Minister). (Courtesy Koes)

42 *Calonarang, bondres.*

43 *Barong Landung*, Kali Ungu, Denpasar.

44 *Cak*, Peliatan. (Courtesy Gen' ichi Tsuge)

45 '*Barong* and *Rangda*', Tourist Performance. (Courtesy Gen' ichi Tsuge)

46 *Rangda*, in the form of a rice-cake offering. (Courtesy Koes)

47 *Barong Ket*, Batik painting.

48 Panji Story, Gambuh dance-drama.

49 Delem and Sangut, Batik painting.

50 Twalen and Wredah, Batik painting.

51 *Baris* Melampahan, Batik painting.

52 *Tumulilingan* (Bumble Bee), Batik painting.

5 Secular Dances in Secular Spaces

IN this chapter a number of Balinese dance genres customarily presented in secular spaces are considered. These dances are usually performed just for recreation and entertainment and are not often put up on occasions connected with religious observances. The genres discussed in the previous chapter such as Legong and Kebyar may also be presented purely for public entertainment, pleasure, and profit outside the context of a religious ceremony, and even bebali genres like Gambuh and Wayang Wong may be performed in purely secular circumstances so long as authentic sacred objects are not employed.

Secular space in Bali is located at an intermediate point on the kaja-kelod axis. Above it are the clearly ranked levels of outer, middle, and inner temple courtyards which rise to the kaja end of the scale. Below it are the dangerous haunts of demons—the graveyard, haunted places, certain crossroads—which lie at the kelod extreme. Secular performances may be presented in a temporary theatre set up in a public square or street, or in a balé banjar (ward association hall), a *wantilan* (arena for cockfighting), or even in a permanent theatre building. Very often nowadays tickets are sold, and the audience is provided with fixed, even reserved, seats. Electric lighting is increasingly common nowadays, but modern theatrical equipment is still rare.

Joged Dances

The several sub-varieties of this group are of great historical importance in Balinese dance, although they have declined considerably in popularity in recent years. The *Joged* (an old Indonesian term, meaning 'female dancer') genre is distinguished by a social dance feature: after the dancer has completed an extended pure dance solo in Legong style, men from the audience are invited by turns to come forward to create a flirtatious improvisation with the skilful performer. Similar 'dance-party' customs, in which men come from the throng to dance one by one with a professional dancing girl, are common also in many other parts of Indonesia, as well as in Bali.[1] *Ngibing*, as the improvisational dancing is called, employs a basic

[97]

vocabulary of movement which is common to modern classical Balinese dance in general, but in ngibing the sensual possibilities of the medium are emphasized: sexy, undulating wriggles, coy gestures with the fan, inviting smiles and suggestive winks are characteristic of the form. Joged is a somewhat denatured survival from a pre-colonial Balinese tradition in which dancing and prostitution were closely linked.

The Dutch scholar, Van Eck, who wrote in 1880, described the public dancers of the period:

After the course of every important cockfight there is for great and small the opportunity to test one's luck at cards or dice. And on these occasions the public girls, or *joged tongkohan* are not lacking; they are sent out by their masters—the princes and headmen—for common account, to save the men and adolescents the trouble of carrying their still remaining coins home. The principal fun consists then in that one, in local fashion, may *ngigel* (dance) for a few minutes with such a joged tongkohan (they are called *ronggeng* in Java). Thereupon there follows another freedom. . . . After the dance has run its course, the dancer separates himself and sits among the many spectators; the girl follows him in order to get her payment, which usually consists of five to six Balinese coins, and for that wretched sum she is obliged to sit on the laps of the dancer and his friends and receive their caresses.

It is disgusting to see how such a girl during half the night is pulled hither and thither and regularly tormented with the kisses and embraces of great and small, young and old, without her being permitted to resist.[2]

According to older Balinese informants, it would not be inaccurate to say that in former times the liberties permitted often went far beyond kisses and caresses. Very often, too, a young boy dressed in woman's costume, called a *gandrung* (see below), danced the solo and received partners from the audience; apparently the substitution did not inhibit the enthusiasm of the male audience for fondling the dancer.[3]

In the past, a payment of money or goods was invariably required from the *ibing*, as the males who come forward to dance are called. In pre-colonial Bali the dancers belonged to the ruling princes, who held a monopoly of the profession, and who received a percentage of the income that came in. Although not all of the royal *penyeroan* (prostitutes) were trained as dancers, those who were able to dance enticingly earned large sums for the princely coffers. The performers were permitted to keep a portion of their earnings, and many were able eventually to purchase their freedom and retire to more respectable lives in the villages, where some of them set up as teachers of the dance. Retired joged dancers became an important factor in the transmission of the forms and standards of performance of the court dance into the village communities.

It would be inaccurate to emphasize too much a distinction between the joged tongkohan and the other female court dancers of pre-colonial Bali. The services of dancing girls (and sometimes boys) were often required in the great households of the rulers; the joged tongkohan were only the lowest in status among them. Above them were the 'private' joged, whose dancing and sexual favours were reserved for the master and his guests. Jacobs, a Dutch medical doctor who travelled in Bali in 1881 on government assignment, reported that performances by joged dancers were presented as part of the official hospitality extended to his party. Jacobs was fascinated by the joged and almost against his will found himself responding to their art:

In the late evening the Prince of Mengwi sent us five *joged tongkohan* from his private collection, Balinese beauties, but of course of blemished virtue. For someone who sees the entrance of various of these ronggeng for the first time it is truly a pleasant appearance and makes, I should almost say, a bewitching impression, to which many circumstances contribute. In the first place, the arena in which the dancing takes place is only sparingly illuminated by a few torches, so that all is wrapped in magical darkness; then the costume which the dancers wear, viz. the drawn-up high, many-colored, tightly-fitting sarong, which with difficulty covers both sides of the bosom, the long, jet-black hair which partially hangs loose, idyllically woven through with crowns of cempaka flowers, the ornamental line-dance which is performed to the soft tones of the gamelan, the naughty, much-signifying glances which they, (on orders from on high, to be sure) throw to the guests in turn; all this together brings the older in years who see it for the first time into rapture for a moment.[4]

Jacobs also reported that the traveller who was the guest of a
Balinese prince for the first time might discover with surprise
that the joged had dawdled after the performance to see if other
entertainment, of a more intimate nature, were required. These
'private' joged do not seem to have performed the ngibing
improvisation with their audiences.[5]

At the top of the hierarchy of court dancing-girls were the
legong, who might be kept exclusively by the princes, and who
were permitted to dance only for them and for guests of high
station. Unlike other dancers, the legong lived in the palace and
were always accompanied—at least when on duty—by a group
of guards armed with ceremonial lances. The dancers, girls of
ten and eleven years of age, had to retire from Legong upon
reaching puberty; it is not likely that they were called upon for
sexual services, nor did they dance with men from the audience.
But as far as orchestra, costume, basic choreography, and
fundamental vocabulary of movement were concerned, the
Joged and Legong were identical. Before the ngibing section of
the performance, the joged even today performs a pure dance
solo in Legong style. The gamelan used for both Legong and
Joged in the courts was the *Semar Pegulingan*, a large ensemble
which is accounted the sweetest of Balinese orchestral ensembles; it is named for the God of Love.[6]

Upon reaching adolescence, the retiring legong might well
have gone on to become a royal concubine and perhaps a joged.
No stigma, however, was attached to the art of dance itself,
despite the association between dancing and the royal harem.
Members of the noble families themselves received dance
training and appeared in performances. Daughters of the prince
often studied Legong, and although they had to give up performing when they reached puberty, some of them later became
teachers of Legong in the palaces.

After the Dutch took power in Bali, efforts were made to
suppress certain aspects of Balinese culture that were repugnant
to the colonialists' sensibilities. Along with the opium traffic,
the burning of widows, slavery, and civil warfare, the prostitution monopolies held by the nobility in the various states

were suppressed. Since the colonial period, princes have no longer 'owned' the joged. Sponsorship of Joged groups, consisting of dancers, musicians, and their helpers, passed over to the ward associations, kin-groups, and to independent clubs (*seka*). In many instances, however, support and encouragement for the groups continued to be offered by the noble families, even after the seka had become public rather than private institutions.

Let us now turn to the various kinds of Joged that survive today. The various sub-genres will be discussed in turn.

Leko

This type of Joged is very closely associated with Legong. It is performed by young female dancers, 12 to 14 years of age, who invariably have previously been performers of Legong. Today Leko is only found in Tabanan Province, where groups exist in Tunjuk and Bongan Jawa villages. The performance opens with a thirty-minute introduction identical to the opening section of the Legong dance. The story of Lasem, complete with the maidservant and bird of ill omen, is represented. The Semar Pegulingan ensemble furnishes the accompaniment; it is played in a very old-fashioned style.

At the end of the introductory section, the ngibing begins. It is accompanied by a special, very lively, composition which is played in fast tempo. Only two of the young dancers perform in this part, one by one. Each of them carries a loose scarf in one hand, and a fan in the other. When the soloist begins this section, men shout from all over the audience, urging her to choose them. Very often the performance will have been commissioned in connection with the six-month birthday of a young child, and the first partner will be the child's father, who dances holding his baby in his arms. Each dancer improvises with several men in turn and then retires while her colleague takes her place. The girl goes out into the audience to select her partner; she designates the lucky man she chooses by tapping him with her closed fan. Once the male reaches the stage, the leko wraps her scarf around his waist, and the two perform

[101]

together for a few minutes. Some men, better dancers than others, are permitted to remain longer than the rest. It is characteristic for the partner to take the lead, and a good joged is esteemed for her skill at following closely and responding deftly to the dance overtures of her partner. The man attempts to get very close to the dancer, perhaps even close enough to kiss her, but the joged always darts away in time to evade him. In Leko today no money is paid to the dancer, and the men are never allowed to take any indecent liberties with her.

Joged Gudegan

Joged Gudegan is known by this name in Sukawati village, Gianyar Province, while in Singapadu village, Gianyar, it is known as *Joged Pingitan*, and in Klungkung it is called *Joged Tongkohan*. All three types descend directly from the dances of the private joged of the Balinese princes of the nineteenth century. The performers are older than the leko—they are perhaps seventeen- to nineteen-years-old. Accompaniment is characteristically provided by a special gamelan ensemble made from bamboo, which is called the *Gamelan Rindik*. This group consists of five pairs of bamboo xylophones in *pelog* tuning, completed by normal percussion and gongs; the repertoire is exactly the same as for Legong.

As in Leko, the first part of the Joged Gudegan performance is pure Legong. In Sukawati village the Lasem story provides the theme, while in Singapadu village Calonarang is the subject of the highly-abstract drama. The ngibing section, however, differs from the Leko. For the introduction, the stage area is brightly illuminated with many pressure lanterns or by electric lighting. When the ngibing is about to begin, these lanterns are quickly removed and are replaced by a sputtering torch, which renders the dancing place much darker, creating a flickering, magical quality of light. The dancer taps her chosen partner with her fan and brings him to the stage area. The dancing begins around the torch, where a kind of seduction is mimicked—the dancers circle the flames of the torch; the joged makes enticing eyes at the ibing, then darts to the other side of the fire when he

[102]

advances, evading him. After three or four such passes around the torch, the couple comes forward to improvise in the same manner as in Leko and other varieties. Three girls perform in turn, each dancer improvising with two or three partners in succession.

In Singapadu village the Joged Pingitan group was formed and taught for many years by a former 'private' joged who served in the Kerajaan Timbul Sukawati, a great palace in former times. This dancer brought with her from the palace an old-fashioned *Gelungan Joged*, the traditional head-dress worn by the joged before the Legong costume was more or less universally adopted. This head-dress, now considered a sacred heirloom, has been passed down through six generations of dancers, who worked under the old teacher and her successor, the late I Madé Kredek. *'Pingit'* means 'secret' or 'selected' and originally designated the joged reserved for royalty; nowadays, because of the association of the word with the sacred head-dress, it has acquired a connotation of 'holy' or 'sacred'. The head-dress itself is a simple holder for a crown of fresh flowers and burning incense sticks, furnished with an elaborately worked and gilded piece covering the dancer's forehead. It closely resembles the head-dress of Rejang.

Adar

This form is no longer performed at the present time, although it cannot be said to be totally extinct, since the expertise needed to perform it still exists, and it may be revived some day. In the 1930s, *Adar* ('enjoyment') groups existed in several villages in Tabanan Province. In Gebug and Kediri villages the performing groups were sponsored by the ward associations, while the groups in Selinsing and Kerambitan were under the sponsorship and patronage of members of the former royalty. The Adar was traditionally offered only at harvest time.

The performance normally would take place in the street close by the balé banjar (ward association hall). Around the dancing area many small stands and stalls for vendors were set up, similar to the arrangement which prevails at any Balinese festival even today, but in this case some of the booths were operated by the seven or eight girls who would take part in the dancing. Before and during the performance, men from the crowd would gather around the tables, bidding for the little items sold by the girls. The men who made the most valuable offers of rice, coffee, cash, or other valuables for the cigarettes, peanuts, or wine would later be selected to dance as ibing. The best offer of all would earn the opportunity to dance first. Remnants, not so vestigial, of the earlier practice of paying for the privilege of dancing may be seen in this custom, which is called *medagang* ('selling'). The same manner of bargaining is still also customary in some villages where prostitutes of the old-fashioned type (who are not dancers) practise their trade. They are paid for sexual favours by accepting greatly inflated prices for small objects of little value. At the Adar performance, men in the crowd, feeling rich with their proceeds from the recent harvest, or with winnings from cock-fights, would bid furiously, inflamed at times with an almost reckless sense of competition, for the right to dance.

The performance took place late at night, and was illuminated by small coconut-oil lamps. Before the dancing began the girls would return from their little vending booths to form a chorus and sing a traditional Balinese folk-song:

> Beautiful brother, come and make enjoyment now!
>> Make your feelings happy right now;
> And if you are as happy as I am,
>> I promise to live and die with you.

The Adar performance contained no introductory dance section. One by one, by the dim light of the lamps, the girls would select their partners and dance in the performance arena for a time. Then the dancer and the ibing might withdraw to the darker shadows, to dance in a more private place. While she was thus away from the stage, her place would be taken by another girl. Adar would go on until very late at night, often continuing until dawn.

[104]

When the girl had finished dancing (and perhaps making other 'enjoyment') with her partner, she might return to her vendor's booth to secure a new ibing for her next turn as dancer. The money brought in by the dancers went to the general fund of the sponsoring organization and was used for community betterment projects. Here village organizations, with or without support from the former royalty, took over what had been a monopoly of the Princes prior to the colonial period.

The independent village groups at Gebug and Kediri possessed only bamboo instruments for the accompaniment of the Adar, but the groups from Selinsing and Kerambitan used the Semar Pegulingan gamelans which had formerly belonged to their high-caste sponsors.

Gandrung

This was also a very important form of Joged that is now all but extinct. In it a young boy took the role of the dancer, and, following a pure dance solo in the Nandir-style (see above), danced with an ibing from the audience.[7] *Gandrung* ('Infatuation') performances in the old style were still given in the 1930s, complete with ngibing. Covarrubias reported at that time that the audience could become very rowdy at a Joged performance, and especially at the Gandrung, which he considered a more 'decadent' form.[8]

Two Gandrung groups in the Denpasar area are still functioning at the present time. In both of them the dancers are young girls, rather than boys. The preliminary dance is pure Legong and employs the Lasem plot. In the second section of the performance a rather stylized ngibing is performed in which the sexual element is not emphasized. The only surviving aspect of the performance specific to the old Gandrung is the musical composition which accompanies the ngibing, called *Gending Gandrangan*. Both these groups perform regularly for tourist audiences and the dancers often 'tap' foreigners in the crowd to come up and participate.

Joged Bumbung

Bumbung is a Balinese word meaning 'bamboo tube' and

refers to the particular musical ensemble which accompanies the dancing. This, like the Gamelan Rindik, is made up of a group of bamboo xylophones, here four in number, that are in *slendro* rather than pelog tuning. Nowadays these instruments are often played, without dancers, in hotel lobbies and in other tourist haunts; the soft and gentle bamboo sound is quite lovely, yet it can easily be ignored; it is perfect Balinese 'cocktail music'.

Among the Balinese Joged Bumbung is the most popular of the surviving Joged types, although it has declined a great deal from its period of highest interest, during the Second World War. Groups can still be found in the Sanur area, Badung Province, as well as in Tegal Tamu, Gianyar; several groups also exist in villages in Jembrana and in North Bali. According to I Nyoman Rembang, Balinese musicologist, the form originally developed in the coffee-growing area in the western part of North Bali, near the Jembrana border.

The group typically includes a half-dozen girls who dance by turns. There is no preliminary pure dance section; the dancers proceed at once to the ngibing, which is considered very bold and flirtatious by Balinese standards. The group receives a fee for the performance, so the dancers do not make individual transactions with the ibing. The costume consists of a simple Balinese blouse and skirt, plus the traditional scarf which is wrapped around the waist. The head-dress consists of golden flowers which are woven into the hair. It is traditional for the joged bumbung dancers to possess love charms, purchased from a specialist, to help increase their allure. The group from Tegal Cangkring, Jembrana Province, had such powerful appeal in the 1940s that at times they had to bring a wooden ox-cart to the performance to carry home all the coffee they had earned.[9]

After Indonesia achieved independence in 1945, the fad for Joged Bumbung quickly subsided in most parts of the island. To some extent it was the victim of a newly prevailing and somewhat moralistic concern for public propriety. Embarrassing connotations were attached to the Joged dances in general, and the number of groups devoted to the form dropped quickly. In recent years, however, a certain pressure has been felt to revive

Joged dancing, in a new role. Unlike such other Indonesian islands as Sulawesi, Sumatra, or Kalimantan, Bali lacks a real social dance tradition. At the ASEAN summit conference held in Bali at the Pertamina Hotel in 1976, a highly-stylized version of the ngibing portions of the Joged dance was introduced as the basis for a new Balinese form of social dancing. A dozen students from the government dance schools danced simultaneously with partners from the audience. In this context the flirtatious element of the dancing was deemphasized and conventionalized—according to witnesses, hardly a trace of the 'naughty' Joged wriggle was to be seen. Nevertheless the guests seemed to enjoy the experience, and subsequently the experiment has been repeated often at official functions. The dancers wear the simple national costume of blouse (*kebaya*) and skirt (*kain batik*); they do not wear a head-dress, but the traditional fan of the Joged is retained. In this practice we see movement in the direction toward the creation of a new, popular, social dance based on traditional, if simplified, Balinese classical dance movements.

Abuang Kalah

Although Bali lacks a strong tradition of participatory social dancing, vestiges remain of some manifestations in the social dance realm, especially in the Bali Aga village of Tenganan, Karangasem Province. There the *Abuang Kalah*, originally a ceremony but now a kind of performance, takes place annually, on the Full Moon of the first month of their calendar. (This falls within our month of February.) The Abuang Kalah was originally something of a game, partly a group social dance, and partly a ceremonial presentation of the eligible young men and women of the village to each other and to the society around them.

The adolescent girls of the village wear the traditional costume of Tenganan, with gold flowers in their hair and the famous *grinsing* cloth skirt, breast-band, and sash. They dance side by side in a stately line, with their arms perpendicular at shoulder height, to the stately tones of the sacred *Gamelan*

[107]

Selonding. Across from them are the young men of marriageable age, wearing skirt and cape, with a dagger (kris) thrust through the belt behind, and a head-dress of Karangasem silk. The young women dance, while the men opposite them wait somewhat shyly; behind the young men are the elders of the village who look on and comment vociferously. At last some of the youths gain sufficient courage to move forward to join the girls in dancing; the boys imitate the movements of the girls in mirror fashion. They must enter the music at a particular cadence point, and if they do not enter correctly, the adult critics shout and the boys must then stop and wait for the next opportunity given by the music. The participants have not had prior rehearsals. The more experienced girls occupy the centre places in the female line, and the younger ones attempt to stay in unison with their more expert colleagues. Many levels of skill and grace are in evidence. After thirty minutes or so the dancing comes to an end. The women retreat to the women's compound, while the young men scatter to their homes.

In recent years the Abuang Kalah has become more of a performance and less a social occasion. The customs of the Bali Aga people are of considerable interest to scholars, tourists, and government officials, and nowadays at the Abuang Kalah event a V.I.P. seating area is set up, with comfortable chairs and refreshments. Many visitors attend, and the participants are on display to a much broader audience than formerly, an audience composed moreover of strangers to the community.

Gebyog

One of the glories of Bali is the extraordinary range and variety of its folk music. Little studied as yet by scholars, especially with respect to the folk-song, Balinese folk *music* far outweighs the folk *dance* in importance. In several instances, however, rhythmic music and secular dancing are closely associated.

Threshing rice by hand is a traditional Balinese domestic task and social activity now growing less common due to the increasing use of machinery for the purpose. But in many places rice is still stored in granaries in an unthreshed state, whence it is taken and prepared for use as needed. When rice is threshed by hand the grains are detached from the husks in long troughs which serve as mortars in which the rice is pounded with tall wooden pestles. Other workers separate kernels from chaff by flipping the pounded mixture up from flat circular baskets; the chaff blows off to the side while the heavier edible grains drop back onto the basket.

Formerly, when a large festival was being prepared for, enormous amounts of rice would have to be threshed in this way, and a large group of people were gathered to do the work. Women did the tossing and pounding, while a smaller number of men lent a hand carrying the heavy baskets of rice. The mood was invariably happy and relaxed, and such a gathering was often the occasion for teasing, gossip, and flirtation. It offered the crowded sense of bustle (*ramai*) that Balinese people enjoy.

Often, as such a group worked, the women pounding at the long mortar trough would start a kind of improvisation, developing a complex interlocking pattern of polyrhythms from the '*byog-byog-byog*' (hence: *Gebyog*) sound created by their falling pestles. The elaborate rhythmic structures resulting are considered by many Balinese musicians to be the source for the patterns used by the Cak chorus accompanying the Sang Hyang Dedari dances.[10] In the cremation or harvest festival context, however, the women would sing a folk-song to the accompaniment of the pounding rhythms, such as 'Crow Steals Eggs' (*Guak Maling Taluh*), 'Moonlight' (*Galang Bulan*), or 'Fisherman' (*Juru Pencar*). Typical lines from the songs might be given thus: 'Let's go and play together in the moonlight' or 'Don't you dare come over and try to steal my eggs; grandpa will be back soon!' or 'Let's go out and catch a great big fish—she'll bring us lots of pleasure later on!' All the songs involved a flirtatious element of double *entendre*, and an invitation to do something together. They were simple choral melodies; some sections were sung in unison, while others were in 'question and answer' form.

While two dozen or more women pounded the rice and created the 'percussion' accompaniment, another dozen or so

[109]

would toss the mixture of rice and chaff in their baskets. The tossing motion caused their upper bodies to undulate with a wriggling movement reminiscent of the movements employed more suggestively in the ngibing improvisation of Joged. As the men carried the heavy baskets from the mortars to the women doing the tossing, they might begin to move in time to the music and then begin to dance as they approached with their loads. As they walked they would strut and wriggle in a flirtatious manner as comic as it was sexy. And the girls would call as the men danced: 'Come on brother, bring your pestle!' Wisecracking and teasing were general. The girls would come out to dance also, one or two at a time, still holding their threshing baskets. They would dance with the boys in ngibing style, with each couple 'performing' for a few minutes. There was no overt caressing or embracing, and the work went on without interruption, although whispered arrangements for a rendezvous could easily be made as the dance went on.

Such 'performances' were common in many parts of Bali until well into this century, especially in connection with cremation ceremonies, although the custom has perhaps by now disappeared altogether. The last occasion known to the authors at which this kind of 'folk' Joged took place was in Sibang, Badung Province, in 1964, although it is entirely possible that unpublicized revivals have taken place since that time. Gebyog singing and dancing were especially prominent in what is now Jembrana Province in west Bali, where it was done in such villages as Batu Agung. The form was also traditionally popular in Karangasem Province.

Cakapung

Like Gebyog, this folk dance genre derives its name onomatopoetically from the sound of its accompaniment, which is a rhythmic vocal sound similar to that produced by the Cak chorus. Two dozen vocalists chant 'pung-caka-pung-caka-pung' in unison to accompany the dancing. Cakapung is a male social dance, done strictly for recreation and amusement. The genre can be found today only in Karangasem Province and on Lombok, which was formerly a vassal state of Karangasem. A performance might take place any evening, during leisure time. The dancers gather at about 7 o'clock at the balé banjar, the ward association hall, a secular space. The men dress in traditional Balinese everyday dress, with a white shirt and simple head-dress (*udeng*). Some of the participants bring bottles of *tuak* (Balinese palm wine), *brem* (rice wine), or arak (rice brandy). Others bring their fighting cocks, in their bamboo baskets.

The men sit down in a circle, informally, on the floor of the balé banjar, with bottles and other paraphernalia close at hand in front of them. One of the participants will pick up a lontar manuscript, containing texts of Macapat songs; these are classical love songs or laments, written in Balinese, which are the staple of Arja, the Balinese opera (see above). The reader sings a sentence from the manuscript to the accompaniment of *suling* (small flute) and *rebab* (spike fiddle). After each line of the song another member of the group speaks for a minute or so, elaborating on the sentence from the song and making it clear to the audience, which may have trouble understanding because of the highly-embellished nature of the melodic setting. The function of the *pengarti* (explainer) is exactly the same as that of the servant-buffoon characters in Arja, except in Cakapung there is no costume or characterization.

As the evening passes different members of the group take over the reading and explaining functions; everyone drinks freely while the singing goes on. Some of the men stroke and groom their roosters, others prepare *sirih* (betel-nut) for chewing. As the men feel the effects of the tuak, arak, and brem the occasion becomes very boisterous; perhaps shouts and arguments develop over the interpretation of the song.

At last someone abruptly stands up. '*Pung!*' shouts the leader, '*Chekapung-chekapung-chekapung!*' The other men join in the chant and several more stand up to dance, some of them still holding their roosters. One or more of the men may have a Jew's harp (*genggong*) in his pocket; he will dance and play at the same time. The movement is improvisational, comic in style, and resembles ngibing without the flirtatious element. Some of the men are trained dancers in established classical dance forms and elements of Baris, Topeng, Gambuh can be seen in their cavorting. A cheering, laughing crowd surrounds the performers. As one dancer gets tired he sits down and is replaced by another. The fun goes on until late in the evening.

Godogan

The genggong mentioned in the preceding section is a Balinese folk musical instrument made from bamboo or palm-leaf. In sound it is similar to the Jew's harp familiar in the West. Genggong is often heard nowadays at Balinese tourist hotels, where it is used to provide a kind of pleasant background music. In Batuan, Gianyar Province, a group devoted to the performance of a particular folk-tale, using genggong accompaniment, was established in 1967 by a well-known Topeng dancer, I Madé Jimat. The tale, 'Godogan', is a Balinese version of the familiar fairy tale about the princess who marries a frog.

I Madé Jimat's group uses a typical set of Topeng masks to present the story. Topeng and Baris provide the vocabulary of movement, supplemented with realistic pantomime in the portrayal of the frog. The frog costume is a modern creation, based on a green jumpsuit. The group performs often, especially at the Sanur hotels.[11]

Janger

Janger is an interesting genre of Balinese performing art which undoubtedly has its roots in old social dance customs no longer in existence. The name can be translated as 'infatuation', with a connotation of someone who is *madly* in love.[12] Unlike Abuang Kalah (see above), which it in some respects closely resembles, Janger is a choreographed, rehearsed presentation. In Janger a variety of elements from many sources—some Balinese, some pan-Indonesian, some Western—are brought together. The genre was created in the early twentieth century, probably in North Bali, although it is not known precisely when.[13]

[112]

Janger has known periods of intense popularity and periods of all but total neglect. Powerful fads of interest in Janger have several times swept over the island, only to suddenly die out until the next revival. Several such waves of popularity occurred in the 1930s as well as in 1965 and in 1974. In the latter instances the outbreaks of the fad happened just prior to periods of political turmoil in Indonesia, and the genre has come to be associated in popular thinking with a season of madness (*musim janger*).

In 1965, during the few months leading up to the attempted Communist coup in Jakarta, Janger groups sponsored by rival political parties sprang up all over Bali; almost all of them disbanded soon after the failed attempt. The revival of 1974 was given momentum when the government sponsored a competition among Janger groups composed of schoolchildren which were drawn from villages in every part of the island. This occurred shortly before disturbances broke out among university students in Jakarta which had troubling repercussions all over Indonesia. The 1974 fad was as shortlived as the earlier ones had been. Today only two permanent Janger groups are in existence, but at any time a new wave of popularity might begin once again.

The distinctive Western features in Janger include certain design elements, especially the painted backdrop, or *tenda*. This scenic element provides the setting for the prologue to the performance and bears a close resemblance to the painted perspective scenery which was common in theatres in the West in the nineteenth century. The same type of realistically painted scenery is commonly found in professional theatres in Java where the dramatic dance form called *Wayang Orang* is presented. The Javanese learned to paint scenery in this fashion from the Dutch.

The male costume in Janger also shows Western influence. It consists of a beret(!), Balinese *bapang* or fancy collar, short trousers, knee-socks, and tennis shoes. Large epaulettes are also included, and some groups have sported uniform sunglasses. These exotic elements and certain other less easily discernible features were taken into Janger from an earlier form of dramatic entertainment, created in Java, known as Stambul, which was seen in Bali early in the twentieth century. Stambul was also the ancestral form that gave rise to the Balinese Drama Gong, a theatrical genre which lacks dance features and therefore is not considered in this volume.[14]

The typical Janger performance begins with a *tableau vivant*, presented in front of the tenda and behind a front curtain (*langse*), which is drawn to the sides to reveal the composition. In a decorative pose the group sings a song in unison, welcoming the audience and requesting their goodwill. In earlier times a master of ceremonies, called the *Daag*, served to introduce and present the group, but this convention has gone out of use. When the opening song has been concluded the langse is closed. The entrance of the twelve men, called *kecaks*, begins the main part of the performance. They march in to the accompaniment of a gamelan composed of gender wayang quartet (as in Wayang Wong), plus rhythmic instruments. Dressed in their short pants, berets and sunglasses, the kecaks execute an elaborate, highly gymnastic, close-order routine involving marching and countermarching, acrobatics, saluting and other movements quite 'foreign' to classical Balinese dancing. But for all its exoticism, the drill quite clearly belongs to the ancient Baris Gedé tradition.

After the male dancers have completed their manoeuvres, they face one another in two rows of six and sit down, forming two sides of a square formation approximately fifteen feet wide. Now the women, who are themselves called janger, enter. They are dressed in traditional Legong costume but wear headdresses resembling those worn in Joged Pingitan. The entrance of the janger is based on the old Rejang processional dance, but the movement is more complicated and reveals a distinct influence of Legong style. As the women dance they sing a folksong in ordinary Balinese, to the accompaniment of chanting and rhythmic sounds made vocally by the kecaks. The first stanza of the song describes the beauty of the janger:

[114]

Someone is coming from the East,
Her costume shines, ornamented with flowers,
Slender is she, with a beautiful forehead,
Whoever sees her falls in love and is filled with joy.

Between the lines of the song nonsense syllables are inserted as part of the musical composition; these are 'si do re si do', based on the syllables of Western solfeggio(!) but sung to the pitches of the Balinese slendro tuning system. The syllables are another legacy from Stambul. The women's dance is slow and very elegant, with much emphasis on fluid, undulating, arm movements; it has nothing of the martial staccato quality of the kecaks' routine. When the women's entrance is complete the janger separate into two lines and also sit facing one another, adjacent to the lines of kecaks, thus forming a square which will serve as the arena for dance-drama which will complete the performance.

But first, two interludes of a musical nature are presented. The first interlude is called *tetamburan* (drumming); in it, as in the entrance of the kecaks, virtuosity is emphasized. The piece is a composition in pure Kebyar style performed by the gamelan and the male dancers, who clap in rhythm and vocalize; they shout the mnemonic syllables employed in teaching Balinese drumming. The section takes its name from a special single-headed drum that is used, the *tambur* (sometimes called *rebana*), which is of Arabic origin. It is about two feet in diameter and is featured prominently in the virtuoso tetamburan display. '*Byung Pyak Be Byung Pyak*' The men clap and chant, while the janger, still seated, move in unison to the rhythm; their movements are drawn from Kebyar Duduk, and the engotan, or side-to-side jerk of the head, is prominent.

The second musical interlude is more lyrical. The male and female semi-choruses sing back and forth to each other in question and answer style. The songs, sung to simple melodies in straightforward rhythm, resemble those described in our discussion of Adar above. After several choruses in a flirtatious mood, the men and women rise and change places and sing again. Finally, after perhaps twenty minutes, a more serious tone is adopted to prepare the audience for the start of the drama, which follows at once. This invariably commences with the entrance of the penasar characters, who begin a performance in typical Prembon or Baris Melampahan style.

Two groups are devoted to the performance of Janger on a permanent basis at the present time. One of them is from Peliatan village, Gianyar Province; this group presents the Arjuna Wiwaha story in Baris Melampahan style. The other group, based in Kedaton, Badung Province, presents the story of Cupak and Grantang, an important Balinese folk story. The principal character is Cupak, a notorious glutton, who eats everything he can get his hands on. In the 1930s this story was itself the subject of a separate dance-drama, notable for the fact that the actor who played the glutton would go into trance during the eating scene and in that condition devour a staggering amount of food. In that performance, as so often in Balinese dance, one could see an old wali element recontextualized, in the same manner as the Sang Hyang Dedari is reframed in Legong. In the Cupak dance-drama it was Sang Hyang Celeng, the trance pig, who reappeared in the frame of the Cupak and Grantang story.[15]

1. Holt (1967), pp. 111−15. See also Raffles (1817, reprinted 1965), I, pp. 340−4.

2. Van Eck (1880), p. 14.

3. Jacobs (1883), p. 14, reported, 'But you know already that they are boys and it disgusts one to see how, at the end, men from all ranks and conditions of Balinese society offer their coins to perform dances in the oddest attitudes with these children, and it disgusts you still more when you realize that these children, worn out and dead-tired after hours of *perpendicular* exercises, are required yet to perform *horizontal* manoeuvers, first stroked by one, then kissed by another.'

4. Jacobs (1883), pp. 186−7.

5. See also Jacobs (1883), pp. 13−14, 56, 101, 112−13, 160.

6. See also Jacobs (1883), pp. 69–70 for a description of Legong in the late nineteenth century palace setting. McPhee (1966), pp. 140–200, treats the Gamelan Semar Pegulingan and related ensembles in detail.

7. Jasper (1902) describes a Gandrung performance he attended at about the turn of the twentieth century; he gives a detailed description of the costume and dancing.

8. Covarrubias (1937, reprinted 1973), pp. 228–9.

9. Private communication to the authors from I Nyoman Rembang, faculty member at KOKAR-Bali, Denpasar.

10. *ibid.*

11. de Zoete and Spies (1938, reprinted 1973), pp. 249–51, describe an interesting performance given to genggong accompaniment in Jimat's village of Batuan, Gianyar Province, in the 1930s and earlier. A frog or toad was also of importance.

12. de Zoete and Spies (1938, reprinted 1973), p. 211, are in error when they define the word as 'humming'.

13. According to the late I Madé Kredek, Janger originated in the village of Menyali, North Bali, and the songs featured in it originally were songs of the horse-cart drivers of that area.

14. Stambul was the creation of a Eurasian Indonesian, named A. Mahieu, toward the end of the nineteenth century. As a high school student Mahieu had read the classics of Western literature in Dutch, and under their inspiration he sought to create a new form of Malay language theatre, accessible to people all over the Malay Archipelago, which was to be a force for their cultural unification. His *Komedie Stambul*, as it was called, made extensive use of Javanese popular music in presenting romantic and fantastic tales from such sources as the *Arabian Nights*. The costumes included the Turkish fez (hence 'Stambul') and other exotic Oriental elements as well as Western features. Mahieu was rather successful and his new genre became popular for several decades. His students established touring companies that travelled widely during the 1920s, and Stambul was performed in Bali, where it influenced Janger, Arja, and Drama Gong. See also Van der Veur (1968), pp. 51–2.

15. de Zoete and Spies (1938, reprinted 1973) describe the Cupak dance-drama, pp. 143–9: they also describe the Cupak and Grantang story as performed in the Janger context, p. 215.

6 'Magic' Dances of the Street and Graveyard

Barong Ket

OFTEN when the moon is full the taruna of Banjar Mukti, Singapadu village, gather at the balé banjar at midnight to take the Barong Ket for a walk. Word passes round in the evening, as the young men return from bathing in the river, 'Come on! We're going out tonight!' The banjar (ward association) owns a magnificent Barong mask and costume, highly charged with magical power, and every few weeks the Club of Unmarried Men is responsible for animating the great mythical figure and taking him around the village to drive off evil spirits.

Many other villages nearby also have Barong; some of them are of the same shape as the stylized lion-face of Banjar Mukti's Barong Ket or *Keket*, while others possess the features of a wild boar, tiger, cow, or even a dog. These types are called *Barong Bangkal, Barong Machan, Barong Lembu* and *Barong Asu* respectively.

Fifteen or twenty young men follow along behind the Barong, which is animated by a pair of dancers, front and rear. The front man holds the mask in his hands and peeps out over it through the great beast's hair. The eight-foot frame of his body is shaggy with white palm fibres, and a little bell and a mirror hang from the animal's tail. No music accompanies the magnificent figure as he trots about the ward, stopping now and again to rattle his wooden jaw loudly. His magical beard, made of human hair, waggles as his jaw clacks at crossroads and village corners, chasing the buta back into the outer darkness. His followers shout their approval.

Sometimes the Barong is in such high spirits from his promenade that he refuses to go home. He and his high-spirited followers pause in front of the balé banjar, uncertain for a moment, and then someone calls, 'He wants to see his girl-friend!' The group takes off at high speed down the road to another banjar half a mile or so away, heading for the storage place of the Barong's friend. The taruna of the neighbouring ward are pressed to bring out their Barong and allow the two mythical beasts, with bells jingling and mirrors flashing, to

[118]

dance a simple pengipuk by the light of pressure lanterns at the crossroad. The followers of the Barong might also find the opportunity to engage in a little flirtation with maidens of the other banjar while they are on the expedition. The entire group makes its way home in time to avoid the sun's first rays.

Every year at the time of the Galungan holiday the young men's club of Banjar Mukti takes the Barong Ket and goes 'on the road' with it, travelling for a week or so from town to town into distant areas. This old custom is called *ngelawang*. They carry all their food with them as well as a small gamelan and camp out along the way. The trip is an annual adventure for the young men of Banjar Mukti, as it is for taruna in hundreds of villages in south Bali.

When the club reaches a new village the gamelan is set up and commences to play, and the dancers in the Barong go through a simple quarter-hour routine. The steps are simple, but the two performers must work together as a single unit. The long-haired beast shuffles and stomps about, and chases the small children in the crowd who dare to approach too closely. When the dance is finished the club is happy to accept a small contribution from their hosts for the good luck they have brought.

Some villagers bring offerings to present to the visiting 'god', while others beg for lucky fibres from the animal's shaggy coat, or for holy water into which the creature's beard has been dipped. Then the group goes on its way to the next village. The expedition is fun for the members and takes them out of their accustomed territory. Following the Barong is a pious exercise that happens also to be an excellent way for young bachelors to meet girls.[1]

The ancestor of the Barong is surely the Chinese Lion Dance, which appeared during the T'ang dynasty (seventh to tenth centuries A.D.) and spread to many parts of Eastern Asia.[2] Originally it seems to have been a showman's substitute for a real 'lion act', performed by itinerant professional entertainers who followed seasonal fairs and festivals. Associated with the Buddha, the Chinese Lion Dance acquired exorcist connotations which it still possesses today. We do not know when the

Indonesian Barong appeared, but it existed in many places in Java as well as in Bali, until the present century.[3]

In the literature about Bali stress has been placed on the Hindu influences which reached the island from India, and less has been made of the important Chinese aspect of the traditional Balinese culture. Relations may have existed between 'Po-li' and China as early as the fifth century A.D., and an eighth-century Balinese king is thought to have had a Chinese wife.[4] A substantial community of overseas Chinese has existed on Bali since before the nineteenth century and remains important today, especially in the world of commerce.[5] Chinese coins (*uang kepeng*) were the traditional medium of exchange on the island, and are important in the making of offerings even now.

All the different kinds of Barong in Bali have exorcist qualities of a magical nature and are thought to be the protectors of the villages. Almost every banjar in south Bali owns at least one of these fabulous creatures, which are regarded as indispensable in the unrelenting war against demons. In addition to the regular bi-monthly patrol which we have described, the Barong is called out when an epidemic or other disaster strikes. His territory is the dangerous places of the community: the graveyard, the crossroad, and the special paths favoured by buta as they go about their troublesome business.

At the time of the Balinese new year, just before Hari Nyepi, the roads of Bali are crowded with processions of Barong on their way down toward the kelod extreme of the ritual axis, the ocean. The Barong are then attempting to drive the buta back into the ocean where they come from and where human beings wish they would stay. The Galungan holiday, an island-wide event, is special to the Barong. People come to the balé banjar to present him with offerings and to thank him for his services during the year.

None of the many different kinds of Barong is given quite as much prestige and respect as the Barong Ket, honoured though the others may be. The mask of the Barong Ket is identical in appearance everywhere it appears and is similar in style to the masks of Wayang Wong. The sekar taji (wing-like leather collar) is also present. It is thought that the masks all descend from a prototype carved and consecrated about a century ago by Cokorda Gedé Api of Singapadu village. Cokorda Api's grandson is still an active maker of Barong masks, in the eighth decade of his life. Today he is the only practising maker of ritually-powerful Barong masks in all of Bali.

According to his account, the *Punggawa* (chief) of Srongga village, Gianyar Province, asked Cokorda Api to make a new Barong, in the form of Banaspati Raja (King of the Woods). 'I don't know what that is', said the mask-maker. 'Come to the *Pura Dalem* (village "death temple") tonight', was the Punggawa's reply. The craftsman appeared at the temple at midnight, and waited in the graveyard nearby to see what would happen. How would the Punggawa test his power? If the artisan did not prove to be strong enough the consequences might be terrible. All at once an unearthly glow appeared in the south-west, at the kelod corner of the temple. An eerie face appeared in the centre of it and the air was charged with power. Cokorda Api made a drawing of the face by scratching the ground with a stick. Subsequently he used the sketch as the prototype for the likeness of Banaspati Raja. Hundreds of examples of the mask have been produced over the years by the members of the Cokorda family.

Already by the end of the nineteenth century the Barong had been brought into a simple form of dance-drama. A Dutch physician, Jacobs, who visited Bali in 1880, saw a performance in which the Barong appeared; the simple story resembled the action depicted in the afternoon section of the Berutuk rite. In it, four masked male figures attempted to carry off four masked females. When the Barong appeared on the side of the women, the males fought it and killed it before carrying the women off-stage. The approach was comic, according to Jacobs, with the masked males striking ludicrous poses and clowning until the fighting section began.[6]

Jauk and Telek

The masked figures reported by Jacobs still exist in Bali today. The males are called *jauk*. They wear a special conical, pointed chandelier-like head-dress in the shape of a Buddhist stupa. The masks are similar in form and bright red in colour. The style of carving and painting resembles the mask of Rawana in Wayang Wong. The face is fierce, with large eyes, shiny visible teeth, and moustache and beard. The dancers wear long artificial finger-nails. The corresponding female characters are called *telek*. Their refined masks are also uniform; they are white in colour with visible teeth, but the expression is pleasant and smiling; these masks are identical to the Sang Hyang Legong masks preserved in Ketewel. The female dancers also wear the identifying pagoda-shaped gelung and carry fans. (In the Sanur area these dancers are called sandaran rather than telek.)

At the present time the jauk dancers are rarely seen in dance-drama, and the telek dancers are hardly to be found at all. Two styles of solo dance for a male dancer clad as a jauk, however, are commonly included in concerts presenting a sampling of different kinds of Balinese dance. Here the format is similar to that of the Baris solo from which it plainly was adapted. In one of them the character is portrayed as 'sweet' and refined, despite his fierce aspect, while in the other the character resembles a puzzled, fierce demon who, it would seem, has been suddenly wrenched into an alien and dangerous reality. In neither case is any kind of story connected with the performance; the form of the solo is taken from the introductory pure-dance section of Topeng. In recent times the Jauk solo has come into service as one of the pengelembar in Topeng Panca or Prembon. It is often included on the bill-of-fare at a revue-style programme presented for tourists.

Rangda (I)

In south Balinese villages it is typical for two examples of a particular, truly remarkable, mask to be kept. This is the fierce mask of long-tongued Rangda, the witch, widely shown in films and books about Bali. One of the two Rangda is customarily kept in the Pura Desa, the village temple, where it serves to protect the village from harm, just as the Barong of various kinds are kept to protect the smaller banjar. The second mask, which like its counterpart is cut from the living wood of the *Rangdu* (kapok) tree and consecrated in a special ceremony, is kept in the Pura Dalem ('death temple'). There it protects the village against the buta who congregate in low, dirty, and dangerous places like the nearby graveyard. In common with every magically-powerful thing, the Rangda mask is regarded with respect and is considered potentially dangerous, but despite its fierce and grotesque appearance the mask is regarded as a benevolent force in the life of the community. It is erroneous to think of her as a devil or even, in the drama, as a villain. The two masks are given the names *Ratu Dalem* (monarch of the temple) and *Ratu Desa* (monarch of the village).

When either temple has its usual Odalan both Rangda are displayed in a special shrine in the temple and offerings are presented to them, along with prayers of thanks and requests for future protection. Often the Barong paraphernalia from the three banjar that make up the *desa adat* (traditional village organization) are also displayed and honoured at the same time alongside them.

Onying

A singular and very striking form of Balinese religious expression is still perpetuated at some Odalan, in which devotees, who are usually elderly women, are 'visited' by the gods and dance in an ecstatic 'trance' state, with daggers and spears. Like the Sang Hyang dancers the devotees often inhale quantities of pungent incense before becoming possessed.

The dancing is orderly enough at the beginning: the step and gestures rather resemble ceremonial Baris. But suddenly, first one, then several, and then all of the dancers are crying and shouting, their bodies taut and shaking with tension. First the kris is extended high in the right hand and brandished, and then the dancer presses it to her chest, straining to stab herself. A few male priests are also among the struggling, shuddering, women. Some dancers hurl themselves to the ground as they try, uselessly, to pierce their bodies with the two-foot kris. They report feeling a rush of 'hot' emotion, and an itching of the skin during the rite.

Priests and older female attendants move calmly among the dancers with bottles of holy water, sprinkling those who need restraint or relief. Adult men in squads surge here and there to help control particularly violent participants. Then, slowly, one by one, the devotees slump limply as the god leaves them. They are carried into a small pavilion to be brought out of trance with additional holy water.[7]

This ritual dance belongs strictly to the wali category. It has no dramatic content. The self-stabbing tests and demonstrates the strength of the god who possesses the dancer; once possessed the dancer is invulnerable to harm and proves it. The same principle applies to the Sang Hyang dancers who run through fire or eat excrement while in the nadi state. The dancer experiences supernatural power and glory, and—for a time—participates in the godhead. The self-stabbing (onying) is not associated with any particular deity, has no particular story, and it is not necessarily associated with any other performance at all. Nowadays, the participants rarely number more than a dozen, but in the nineteenth century reliable observers told of seeing entire villages of 500 people—men, women, and even young children—participate simultaneously in the rite.[8] As a mode of religious expression it reminds one of snake-handling and other such 'charismatic' Western practices.

The Wong Sakti

Thrill-seekers in every culture enjoy watching someone brave take a great risk before their eyes and live to tell the tale. Balinese audiences are no exception, although the island lacks any tradition of wire-walking, high-diving, or other dangerous athletic tricks. But in the realm of magic, black and white, there are specialists who will perform feats before your very eyes. We may call these professionals *Wong Sakti* (men of power). The demonstration involves a contest, either with the ambient spirits in a dangerous location, or with another magician. In 1976, for example, a sensational duel took place between two famous Wong Sakti: one was from Sanur, Badung Province, and the other from Blahbatuh. At that time thousands of spectators gathered on the beach at Sanur to watch great bolts of fire and clouds in the form of giant warriors fly back and forth across the sky.

Apart from the great sorcerers who work on a cosmic scale are many other Wong Sakti who work at a more local level. Certain dalang, for example, who specialize in a certain kind of shadow play, the *Wayang Calonarang*, acquire a reputation for being able to counteract the power of black magicians and other people who can turn themselves into *leyak* (demons). When such a dalang performs, the story he presents exists merely to provide a context for him to challenge local sorcerers to fight him with their magic. 'LEEEEEYAAAAAK!' he cries, forcing them to come forth whether they want to or not. Small blue lights then flicker in the dark street and in the graveyard where the brave dalang gives his performance to show his strength.[9] In the past the Wayang Calonarang might well have been intended as a special rite of exorcism for a household compound or other place troubled by spirits, but now it is a contest, and if local sorcerers are in short supply an expert can be brought in for a fee to ensure an exciting match.

Another professional showman belonging to the Wong Sakti category is the *dusang* (corpse). This man's specialty is playing dead in dramatic performances. He lies inert as he is stripped, washed, and wrapped, while songs for the dead are sung. Then the ceremony for someone newly deceased is carried out before the 'body' is carried to the cemetery and left by itself. To submit to this procedure is considered extremely dangerous, for by doing it the person invites any leyak which may be in the vicinity to come and devour him. The dusang, like the kris-dancer, feels the exaltation of being invulnerable in dangerous circumstances.

Rangda (II)

In Kesiman village, Badung Province, about 2 miles from Denpasar, is *Pura Pengrebongan* (meeting temple), a place of worship sacred to the masks of Barong and Rangda. Its Odalan is famous all over Bali for the cock-fights held in connection with the festivities; all the big gamblers and lovers of fighting cocks attend it, and a great deal of chicken blood is shed. The occasion is always host to a great gathering of the Barong and Rangda from the villages nearby. Thirty or thirty-five of the powerful masks are there. All kinds of Barong are there, as well as more than a dozen Rangda. The great gathering takes place in the jeroan; this is the only time the Barong ever enter that area. With their followers gathered around them, the mighty masks and costumes are set down on the ground, while prayers are offered to the goddess of the temple. Tension mounts as the prayers continue—concentration of energy in the space is enormous.

The pemangku offers a prayer: 'Mother, all of your children have already arrived in your presence. Now please behold them, your loyal children, and give them a sign of your favour!' And suddenly the entire courtyard is seething with struggling men in a state of trance, as the masks are lifted onto their bearers and are brought to life. Thirty-five Barong and Rangda rush out of the temple, pursued by their followers, many of them deep in trance. Barong and Rangda circle the cockpit in a counter-clockwise direction for hour after hour, while many of their loyal followers practise onying, the ritual of self-stabbing. None of the groups interacts formally with any of the others, and there is no story or even dramatic situation.

The concentration of power in the courtyard and the descent of the goddess into her 'children' brings on the same onying possession experienced by the old women described earlier. The young men who follow the Barong are stronger than the old women and their gyrations with the kris are more acrobatic.

[126]

Each dancer has a personal style of doing the stabbing—some lean back, bent almost double with exertion, while others throw themselves to the ground with two kris pressed point first to their eyeballs. The participants are rarely injured. The buta, presumably gorged with blood shed for their benefit at the cock-fight, are driven forth by the horrendous din. Another purpose of the event is the reconsecration of the powerful masks by the descending goddess. At the end of the ceremony the masks and their bearers can return home, ready once more to protect the villages which own them.

At this event and others no special qualifications are required to wear the Barong mask, provided one is a member of the banjar group which owns it. To be sure, the physical requirements are very demanding, especially for the dancer at the front, who must hold the heavy mask and clack the jaws while dancing. If the 75-pound frame is carried for a long period, as it often is during Galungan, the members of the seka taruna take turns in shouldering the heavy burden. When Barong Ket dances to the accompaniment of his gamelan he follows an established choreographic pattern, shaking from side to side, walking quickly, turning back to admire his tail; his eyes flick to the left and right and the jaws rattle in different rhythms. The choreography is rather complicated, and at least basic training in the modern Baris dance style is required.[10]

When the Rangda mask appears in a performance, however, it is a different story. Few of the men who dare to wear the great head and padded costume have had any dance instruction, for Rangda does not need to keep time to the music. She advances into the playing area with a high pouncing step and stops, cackling. Then she arches over in a backbend, shrieking with high, piercing laughter; her hands flutter and her 6-inch fingernails rattle together. She waves in one hand a magical white cloth with secret 'power' symbols drawn upon it. When the mask is not in use, it is wrapped in her dangerous kerchief.

Far more important than technical ability for the man who dances Rangda is spiritual power; this performer must be a Wong Sakti or a priest. Whenever the Rangda mask appears in

[127]

public great forces are unleashed among the people and the other dancers. When Rangda appears, the presence of the deity may be felt so intensely that many in the crowd may fall into trance, almost automatically. The association between Rangda and falling into trance is so close that in some villages if someone goes into trance for any reason Rangda will be sent for, if she is not already present. Certain dancers, all men of great spiritual power, have made a specialty of playing Rangda, and are called when a village wishes to sponsor a performance in which the mask will appear. Always in this case the local sacred mask will be worn by the visiting specialist. It is common for someone to be both a dusang and a Rangda dancer, for both require the same kind of power.

In Balinese classical literature are a number of Kawi epic poems in which principal characters, when enraged, change suddenly into *pamurtian*, which are gigantic, terrifying supernatural manifestations with thousands of heads and arms brandishing weapons.[11] Wisnumurti, for example, is commonly mentioned, for Kresna is an incarnation of Wisnu, and in a number of favourite *Mahabharata* stories he and his opponents change into pamurtian to fight. Pamurtian puppets were designed for the wayang theatre, where quick transformations of appearance can be made easily; the many-armed pamurtian are admired by wayang audiences, because their struggles have a majestic dimension that even on the small screen adumbrates the mightiest forces.

Transformations of appearance are also convenient in Balinese masked theatre, for the performer can make an almost instantaneous change. In Wayang Wong, for example, Rawana takes on the appearance of a brahmana in order to trick Sita, and in the same story Marica is transformed into a supernatural deer. A conventional way to indicate a magical transformation of appearance has evolved: the dancer stops whatever he or she is doing, assumes a special 'meditation' pose, and then withdraws; a substitute dancer takes the first one's place, assumes the same pose, and thus establishes that the original character has been transformed by magic.

[128]

In Balinese dance-drama the special ten-headed, many-armed representations of pamurtian figures found in the Wayang Kulit do not exist. Whenever a powerful manifestation of a god or supernatural being is called for, the Rangda mask is customarily employed. Thus in the *Arjuna Wiwaha* presentation of the Peliatan group, the Rangda appears, to represent the aspect of the highest god, Siva. Even in this highly professional and experienced company, which has performed all over the world, a priest is retained to look after the mask and to dance in it. Rangda functions as the pamurtian of Balinese dance-drama and represents the awful face of divinity, without respect to gender or to character. In the old Balinese story *Basur*, the male sorcerer also assumes the Rangda aspect, when he is working his charms.

The sacredness of the Rangda mask, the Barong outfit, and the likewise holy Sidha Karya mask is not a matter of appearance, for these faces, regarded as visual motifs, are commonly used in many secular applications in Bali; indeed the mask-makers feel no reservation about making and selling perfect copies of the sacred masks to tourists or others. What gives the mask its power is the consecration it receives from its maker, the sacred letters inscribed within it, the holy wood it is made from, and the 'charge' of taksu or *pasupati* it receives in the temple or the graveyard. A holy mask literally manifests the divinity, and whenever one is introduced into a performance the unpredictable can always happen.

Dance of the Sisya

After she had taken the book, she arrived at the graveyard, accompanied by her *Sisya* [apprentices], at a place in the shadow of a *kepuh* tree. . . . There the widow of Girah sat down, ringed around by her students. . . . 'Come! Strike up your musical instruments and let us dance one by one. I will attend to your every movement, and soon when the time for action comes you must all dance together.' Immediately Guyang began to dance: she danced with outstretched arms, clapped her hands, and lowered herself to the ground, twirling her skirt around her—her eyes bulged out and she shook her head to left and right. Then Larung began to dance—her movements were like the tiger when he prepares to attack. Her eyes were red and she was naked. Her hair hung loose in front of her. . . .

Calonarang MS (16th century)[12]

The highest rank of magical power is achieved, not by those who merely purchase a protective amulet, or who get it through some bit of luck, but by those who study under expert teachers able to interpret ancient magical books written in the old Balinese characters. Traditional Balinese medicine has been conducted by *balian*, doctors knowledgeable about herbal remedies and magic spells as well as Chinese apothecary principles. Today certain mountain and coastal villages, like Sanur, Badung Province, are famous for their sorcerers and witches, who practise magic, white and black, and who sell charms and amulets at retail. The most famous of them take students, who are clients desiring to increase their powers. These are sisya, the sorcerer's apprentices.

Black magic may have come to Bali in the tenth century A.D., when Tantric rites from Java were introduced on the island.[13] At that time a Javanese princess named Mahendradatta married the Balinese King, Udayana, who according to tradition later cast her off for practising black magic. To the modern Balinese, Mahendradatta has become an archetype: she is the domineering wife who controls her pitifully weak husband through black magic. Her legend has become inseparably entwined with the old Tantric Hindu-Javanese story, *Calonarang*, which tells of a matron, the Widow of Girah, who is a terrible witch, owner of two very powerful magical books. She tries to destroy the entire country by means of an epidemic spread by magic, for no man dares to marry her daughter. When Calonarang is angered she becomes a pamurtian: fire shoots from her eyes and nostrils, and she takes on the appearance of a monster.

Calonarang's favourite technique is to go with her students at midnight to the crossroads, a magically dangerous place, and there to dance naked until the goddess Durga gives them the power to change into leyak, hideous familiar spirits who fly about the country working mischief and spreading disease. Leyak are still greatly feared in Bali today, and almost everyone has had some personal experience with one. The apprentice black magician receives a charm from the teacher, enabling the adept to take the form of a monkey, goat or other animal. More advanced sisya learn to become smoke or a little point of blue light, or even—at a very advanced level, a huge cremation tower. The peak of achievement, reached by very few, is to attain the power to become Rangda herself, without need of mask or costume.

Black magicians in Bali are business people, and their wares must be publicized. The enterprising have kept up with the times. In 1975 a leyak in the form of a riderless motor cycle was the talk of night-time Denpasar, and at the finish of the famous battle of magicians at Sanur in 1976, the crowd reported seeing a magical aeroplane, absolutely silent, stunting just above the crests of the waves of the surf.

Naked witches no longer dance at the crossroads at midnight in Bali, if indeed they ever did, but the vocabulary of movement described in the *Calonarang* manuscript has survived in the *Igel Sisya*, a product of a little known esoteric dance tradition. We shall describe the particulars of the dance presently. Claire Holt has commented that the dancing described in *Calonarang* is an inversion of classical Balinese dance: the extended arms, loose hair, immodest and uncontrolled gestures, and nakedness are all antithetical to the deepest essential sensibility of classical Balinese dancing.[14] The dance at the crossroads is an equivalent in choreographic terms to reading the scriptures backward, as the black balian do to work an evil spell.

Calonarang Dance-drama

The troubled period around the turn of the twentieth century was a difficult one in Bali, but it was also a time of great artistic energy. The Kebyar 'explosion' of the 1920s only represented the crest of a wave of innovation and new creation begun thirty years or so earlier, when many new subjects, never before represented in the Balinese dance-theatre, were dramatized. Various elements of performance from separate genres were combined and recombined in the staging of new stories, made into new dance-dramas. We have previously seen that Parwa and Topeng Panca were also products of the turn of the century. None of the new forms created was to achieve so great a fame and leave so indelible an impression in Bali and all over the world as the Calonarang dance-drama, created about 1890 in the Batubulan area of Gianyar Province.

Like other Balinese creators, the makers of Calonarang drew from a general cultural pool of pre-established materials. Composition was a process of assembly and arrangement of inherited or given motifs and motifemes (atomic units of action). In common also with other performance varieties, the new form exhibits elements drawn from a wide variety of sources within Balinese culture, some of them belonging specifically to 'the dance', while others are drawn from far and wide in the heritage. At the heart of the new creation is (as is so often the case in the Balinese dance), an attempt to rework a wali element in terms of classical Hindu-Balinese style and conventions.

The Sang Hyang Dedari dancer has been caught, set, and embellished in the Legong; the Baris Gedé has been captured in modern Baris; and Rejang is represented in the Panyembrama. Similarly the Calonarang dance-drama attempts to provide a frame in performance for the Rangda. A crucial difference is that the godhead manifesting in the mask cannot be contained by any human agency, for Rangda cannot be fully tamed.

The places of performance are the graveyard and the crossroad: two areas that are home to buta, at the kelod extreme of the sacred geographical orientation. A kalangan is set up at the centre of the intersection, where paths used by buta and leyak meet and cross. The graveyard and crossroad are also the sites favoured by the witch and her pupils in the old Kawi story. The stage area itself is similar to the kalangan set up in temples; it is

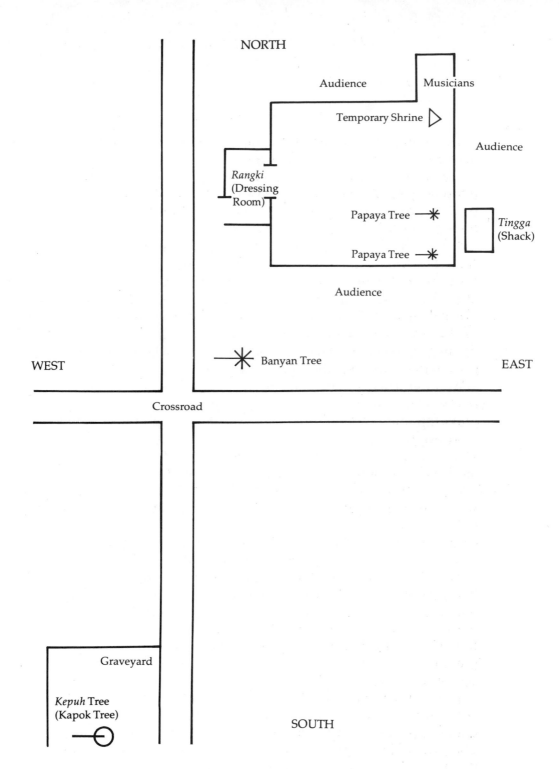

4. Layout of Calonarang Performance

perhaps 18 feet wide and 30 feet deep. The five-toned gamelan Semar Pegulingan is set up to one side.

The special features of the Calonarang stage include a small temporary sanggah (shrine), made of bamboo, which is placed in the corner. The sanggah is identical to the shrines set up outside every Balinese household compound on the day *Kajeng Kliwon*, which occurs every fifteen days on the Balinese calendar. At this time small meat offerings are set out to placate the buta, and it is said that people who like to become leyak pray at such a shrine before going out to make the transformation. The kalangan is also furnished with a small papaya tree, symbol of the great sacred Kepuh tree which grows in nearly every Balinese graveyard. The crossroad itself is usually shaded by a great Banyan tree, symbolic of shelter.

At the end of the space, shut off by a brightly coloured curtain, is the *rangki*, or dressing area, where the dancers put on their make-up and masks. Entrances are made through the curtain. At the opposite end of the stage is another small shack, on stilts, towering high over the space and reached by a precarious ladder. From here Calonarang makes her entrance, as do her sisya. Later Rangda comes down the ladder also. The spectators watch from three sides of the enclosure. This playing space is a half mile or so from the graveyard in which the play will conclude. As always, the kalangan is consecrated before the performance by a pemangku, with libations and a small offering.

The play begins with a series of pengelembar. Very often the Barong Ket from the local banjar will dance, operated by invited dancers from distant villages and cities. Perhaps three different pairs will animate the great beast, demonstrating their virtuosity; here the Barong's followers play no role, and the skill of the dancing is an important concern. Then a Baris dancer may perform, if one is available, followed by a jauk and a telek; each dances a fifteen-minute solo in modern style. The jauk and telek enter from Rangda's elevated shack (*tingga*) to show their skill at dancing down a swaying ladder in mask and heavy costume. The jauk and telek are vestigial descendants of the characters in the type of folk play described by Jacobs in 1880; they are historically associated with the Barong.

The play itself begins with the appearance of the Condong, who in this drama is usually portrayed by a man. The igel ngugal she dances upon entering is identical to the Condong's solo in Gambuh, although minor influences from Arja are clearly visible. The Condong soliloquizes, explaining the background of the story: no one will marry Calonarang's daughter, Ratna Manggali. The young woman then appears, and as might be expected, she is of the same type as the Putri from Gambuh. Ratna Manggali dances and sings before engaging the Condong in dialogue. Why doesn't she have any suitors? The Condong suggests that Calonarang may know the reason. But again following the established Gambuh structure, the subordinates must first appear to make ready for the principal's entrance. The Condong calls the sisya.

Four to six female dancers usually dance in these roles. Their costume is absolutely unique in Balinese dance-drama: the sisya wear half-length white skirts, with a yellow top made by winding a long sash around the dancer's upper body, leaving shoulders and arms bare; the hair is long and hangs loose. Here, in their first appearance, the sisya do not perform a special choreography but dance a simple variant of the kakan-kakan routine described in the chapter on Gambuh. As they dance they call to one another in the Kawi language to make ready. Finally, all take their places, kneeling in a ring on the ground.

Now Matah Gedé appears. This name, which is applied to the Widow of Girah, literally means 'the great uncooked one', referring to the fact that fire has not yet come forth from her eyes and nostrils. The role is played by a male priest. The character wears a white head-cloth and skirt; often a lucky cloth of kain poleng (checkered cloth) is wrapped around her shoulders and she carries a staff on which to lean as she walks.

Calonarang clambers down the ladder and enters the circle of respectful sisya. The vocabulary of movement is pantomimic rather than choreographic, and resembles the movement of the Tua from Topeng. Ratna Manggali greets her respectfully, but then begins to weep:

Condong (translating for Matah Gedé)

Don't be full of sorrow, my daughter, even though no man has
come to ask for your hand. The goddess Durga has looked with
favour on our requests, and has given us permission to punish
the people here in the Kingdom of Daha. As you can see, all of my
sisya are spreading disease wherever they can. I want you your-
self to lead the sisya from now on. Now all of you, listen as I
explain what we will do.

Now the Matah Gedé explains in Kawi how the magical
ceremony is to be conducted and what each of the sisya must do
and become. The Condong translates and elaborates in Balinese. The role of the Condong is considered to be a dangerous
one, because her explanation tells both how to work magic and
how to combat it; for each kind of leyak the proper formulae and
antidotes are explained. This requires the knowledge of the
magician's art contained in certain sacred manuscripts. Local
sorcerers are said to hate the Condong's explanation, for it tells
the public how to ward off their tricks, and therefore the dancer
is thought to be in danger of attack by leyak at this time. This is
the first challenge of the performance. When the scene ends
Matah Gedé and her followers retire up the ladder into the
tingga.

Now the second meeting of the performance takes place. The
penasar serving the King of Erlangga enter; Punta and Kartala
may improvise a comic routine lasting as long as an hour before
they come to the particulars of the exposition: the King is
concerned about the epidemic in his country and plans to send
the Patih to solve the problem by killing Calonarang with a
special kris. The format of the scene is a replica of that of
Topeng. The King enters, dancing his introductory solo, which
duplicates the igel ngugal of the evil Prabu in Gambuh. His Patih, called the Pandung, appears at once, without an introductory
solo. By this odd bit of type-assignment it is made clear that the
King and his ministers are the villains of the performance.

In the Calonarang dance-drama the Pandung is one of the
performers who must have special protection against the danger

of leyak; very often he wears a protective amulet, purchased from a magician. This character will later attack the Rangda with a kris, and he is vulnerable to destruction for his temerity. The dancer who plays this role must undergo a ceremony (mawinten) in which he is consecrated to the part. The characterization is exactly that of the Prabangsa from Gambuh; his costume is taken from the arya-arya in the older form.

The brief scene between King Erlangga and his Patih is interpreted by the penasar. The Prabu instructs the Patih to go to kill Calonarang, accompanied by the two servants. Now begins the pangkat (formal departure). The three emissaries travel back and forth across the stage a few times, describing the scenery they pass as they travel. They stop several times to search out the correct path. After a while the trio 'arrives' at Girah. The penasar comment on how ugly the vicinity looks, and how terrible it smells thereabouts. 'Let's wait over here!' They exit to the rangki (dressing area).

Now the pressure lanterns are dimmed, and some of them are removed by members of the gamelan, who do double-duty as stage-hands. The central scene is about to take place. This is the Transformation, in which the sisya dance at the small shrine and before the papaya tree. Their singular choreography has descended no doubt from Tantric rites such as those described in the old *Calonarang* manuscript.

Although traces of Legong style are found in the sisya choreography, especially during the entrance, the basic vocabulary of movement is entirely unique in Balinese dance. The girls cover their faces with pieces of white cloth, their loose hair hangs free in front. Some of them immediately begin to mime picking up dead babies from the ground, while they all howl with laughter. Dolls wrapped in white cloth provide very realistic properties. The sisya mime eating the little bundles, and then they dance again, shaking their breasts obscenely and jumping from side to side while in a squatting position. They wiggle their buttocks with an ugly motion. In general it may be said that they defy every customary aesthetic principle of Balinese dance. At the end of their ten-minute routine, the sisya sit down on the ground to await the entrance down the ladder of Rangda. This is the Widow as pamurtian.

Her dancing during the igel ngugal at first centres around the little papaya tree in the kalangan. She searches for it and stops to shriek with glee when she finds it. She rubs her back against the little plant, symbol of her own pohon kepuh (graveyard tree). Then, satisfied, waving her cloth and laughing in a unique snorting high-falsetto, she inspects her students. 'Now daughters, go and kill all the people in Daha. Let not one remain alive! Go to each of the nine directions!' The sisya scatter and disappear; Rangda, shrieking with delight, clambers back up the ladder to her house, accompanied by the Condong.

At this time the chief comic scene of the performance takes place. It is performed by bondres (comic villagers and comic leyak). The audience always finds this scene hilarious, although the joking is in a distinctly macabre, almost ghoulish, vein. The rustics, five in number, enter with a (property) dead baby, wrapped for burial. They carry torches to light their way to the graveyard. All five wear simple, bold, comic make-up; some carry farming implements. The woman in the little cortège is crying, while the men sing a mournful dirge.

The procession pauses for a moment, when suddenly Pang-pang—Rangda's chief assistant—appears with two lesser comic demons. The scene becomes quite slapstick. A favourite section depicts one of the stupid bondres who fancies himself a black magician. He intones imitation mantras, sits in imitation meditation, and then imitates entering trance. Unbeknownst, Pangpang creeps up from behind, and afflicts the rustic with vomiting. After an hour or more of clowning, after chasing and beating each other in the confusion, the bondres drive off the comic demons and then the dusang enters.

At this moment in the performance the mood of the audience changes sharply. The mothers and fathers clasp their children to them, as the Professional Corpse walks in and lies down on his pallet made of bamboo. He makes no attempt to enact a character, or to feign illness. He simply walks in, and the crowd becomes sombre and tense. The bondres strip off his clothes,

[138]

except for a loincloth, wash him, place Chinese coins on his eyes, and cross his arms. Then offerings for the dead, authentic in every particular, are presented. An older actor prays while the others chant the liturgy for the dead. Then they pick up the pallet and proceed down the road by torchlight, singing a dirge, to the (real) cemetery. Some members of the audience accompany the procession, while others wait at the crossroad for the climactic and most dangerous moment of the performance, the attack of the Pandung on Rangda.

The Pandung enters the stage area with his attendants. One of the clowns creeps silently up the ladder and peeks into the Widow's shack and then returns. The Pandung resists the idea of attacking a sleeping enemy, which his servants urge him to do, but he yields at last to their persuasion. He mounts the ladder and steps inside for a moment, then drags out Rangda and hauls her, kicking, down the ladder, stabbing furiously with his magic kris. The dancer *literally tries* to kill the Rangda, but is prevented by the magical power of the mask and that of the man who dances it. Rangda laughs and exults, and quickly chases the Pandung off the stage. In the old story, Calonarang burns him to death with fire that comes from her eyes and nostrils and mouth, but this is not represented in the play.

The dancer performing Rangda is now at a peak of excitement, and may have entered a state of trance. He now begins to challenge the leyak to attack him personally. In the context of the story, Calonarang as Rangda, in a transcendental state of anger, is here, calling her sisya to join her for further depredations on the countryside. But more literally, the dancer at this moment invites and dares all local practitioners of the dark arts to test his power. The performance moves at a double level of being, in which almost contradictory messages are expressed. Rangda dances in character all the way to the graveyard, shouting her challenges, while the remaining spectators follow at a respectful distance. Sometimes the dancer of Rangda feels so exultantly invulnerable that he strips off the mask and invites the leyak to attack him personally: 'All you leyak come on! Attack me all together! ME! Attack ME!'

[139]

The audience has been disappearing steadily since the dusang appeared, as the more timid members of the audience decide to go home. The crowd continues to thin out as the group approaches the real graveyard, with its massive rangdu tree. Only the older, braver, members of the community follow the dancer into the cemetery, where he repeats the summons and challenge. The members of the gamelan have followed, however, and are now eager for the performance to come to an end. They struggle to bring the exalted dancer under control, and the pemangku assists them. By now the members of the company are eager to reach the safety of their homes as soon as possible. Rangda is wrestled to the ground and the dancer is doused with holy water. They drag him off to the banjar temple nearby to restore him to his normal condition. The beard of the Barong Ket is dipped into the holy water to give it special strength; the dancer gulps down this restorative and wipes it over his face and upper body to purify himself from the recent experience. Then all go to their homes.

All, that is, except for the dusang, who lies motionless in the graveyard, alone. There he will remain until shortly before the sun rises, invulnerable to all the leyak of the area. No one usually dares to stay to watch with him. He will return to the banjar around dawn: 'Hey, where's my shirt? What kind of cowards are you?' The dusang is entitled to brag a little, for he has run a hideous risk. The performance is over.

Calonarang dance-drama is still popular in South Bali, especially in the Gianyar and Badung Provinces. The villages of Pagutan, Den Jalan, Tegal Tamu, Singapadu, and Celuk—all in Gianyar Province—still maintain companies complete with 'sacred', Rangda and Dusang. However, the Calonarang production at ASTI-Bali in Denpasar, seen by many tourists, contains no sacred elements. In the village setting, the performance is given on the occasion of certain Odalan at the banjar temple where a Barong Ket is kept. Traditionally it had a different function.

In Calonarang as in Topeng Pajegan ritual elements (wali) are embedded intact among more secular features. No fewer than *five* members of the company must have special spiritual powers or defence. The Pandung may be protected by an amulet purchased from a balian, whereas the Condong and the Matah Gedé must be literate and have specific magical knowledge. The dusang is given his power by the gods directly, but it may not last for more than a few years. In several villages he is the pemangku at the Pura Dalem. And Rangda is a professional specialist. Two very active Rangda dancers of the present time are Cokorda Alit, a very powerful man of the *ksatrya* caste from Blahbatuh, and I Madé Kengguh, of Singapadu, a musician, dancer, and expert teacher of the dance of Rangda. These men are often invited to perform with groups from villages in which a man strong enough to 'carry' the deity is lacking.

The Calonarang dance-drama was formerly a specific remedy against evil sorcery, and the play—like the Wayang Calonarang—can still be applied to this purpose. In this respect, the Calonarang repertoire is quite distinct from ceremonies to chase or propitiate the buta, who are 'natural' demons rather than malevolent humans in transformed shape. It would be preposterous to cleanse a graveyard of buta, for such beings can never be destroyed, but only displaced, and if they were driven from the graveyard they would enter the village and rice-field. The Balinese do not hold cock-fights, offer *caru*, or pour libations—all measures to control the buta—in the graveyard. A buta in the graveyard is where it belongs, if it is not in the ocean.

The Calonarang play was created to counteract and neutralize the supernatural power of black magicians who are *specific* individuals in the community. The headquarters for magic, black and white, is located in a small number of coastal villages, like Sanur, Ketewel, Matolan, and Lebih, situated at the kelod extreme of Bali across from Nusa Penida, the traditional haunt of devils. As befits black magic, the principal ingredients in sorcerers' concoctions consist of products associated with the sea, such as fish oil and bones, and seaweed. Inland practitioners of the evil arts must get their medicines from the coastal balian, and hence their identities and preferred potions can be discovered through astute detective work.

[141]

In the performance of the dance-drama the Condong plays a key role: it is she who explains to the public *who* is practising *what* kind of magic, and how their spells can be counteracted. Then the Rangda and the dusang challenge the magicians to throw their worst at them. When the Rangda dancer and dusang survive unscathed at least a temporary respite from sorcery has been won. In the Wayang Calonarang the roles of *namer* and *challenger*, each requiring special powers, are gathered into one performer. But in the Calonarang dance-drama the functions are shared among the five specialists.

In the light of this very specific function certain perplexities become clear. One source of misunderstanding arises from the fact that the performance concludes with the triumph of Rangda. In Balinese theatre it is highly unusual for any drama to conclude with the victory of the evil party. In fact we might think of the narrative in Balinese drama in general as a means by which the struggle between the good and evil parties and the final victory of the good can be contextualized. In a sense *all* the stories exist only to provide given circumstances for the ritual battle. In Calonarang, Rangda is the *heroine* of the performance and represents the protection of the village against the sorcerers. Although the play concludes very early in the old Javanese story which is its source, it has reached the perfectly appropriate conclusion. Since Rangda is the village protector it is no wonder that the Balinese find it difficult—if not impossible—to represent her defeat in the theatre.

Barong Landung

A final type of magically protective effigy is the *Barong Landung*, which is found in many villages of the Denpasar area in preference to Barong Ket and to the other·types of animal Barong. 'Landung' means 'tall', and indeed the 10-foot figures tower over their bearers and attendants. These effigies have human faces and features.

Five of them comprise a complete set: Jero Gedé (the big man), Jero Luh (his wife), and their three children. The Luh has

Chinese features and yellow skin while her husband has a black complexion, long hair and fangs; he is said to represent a Dravidian from ancient India. The children are of somewhat shorter height and wear masks which remind the viewer of those used in telek.

Barong Landung, like the other Barong types, is a possession of the village. The dancers are drawn from the strongest young men, who alone can handle the size and weight of the giant figures, each of which is carried and operated by a single performer. During most of the year Jero Luh and Jero Gedé and their children remain in the home banjar, but at Galungan time they appear on the highways of the Denpasar area in the evenings. At this time groups with a set of Barong Landung figures walk from village to village, dancing and singing Balinese songs, to the accompaniment of the gamelan batel.

When the procession reaches the balé banjar of the village to be visited, a small circle of spectators gathers around the milling figures. There a simple domestic drama in the Balinese language is enacted in song and speech; the subject is drawn from daily life. The play contains jokes and comic business, along with bits of homely good advice from parents to children. The husband and wife quarrel and argue for a short time, but there is no fighting sequence. The little play concludes with songs by the principal characters, and then the procession moves along to the next village.

Procession During the New Year

Once every fourteen months the Balinese celebrate their New Year holiday, called Hari Nyepi. This is a time of cleansing and renewal, a time to clear up old debts and a time to be reunited with members of one's family. On Hari Nyepi it is the rule to stay home quietly. Older people fast and meditate, and no one is permitted to make any loud noise. New Year's eve, however, is a very lively occasion. In many villages noisy purification rites designed to frighten away the *buta* are held, and every family sets out large offerings for the buta outside their houseyard. In a sense the entire island is to be swept clean of demons on this day.

To help accomplish the purpose, the gods in their small pratima figures and the Barong of various kinds are carried in procession on the roads by all the active temple congregations on the island. On this day it seems that everyone in Bali is on the march with umbrellas and banners and marching gamelan, going in procession down the highways and byways to the sea or to a river that leads to the sea. Every banjar, village, kin-group, and irrigation society takes to the road, dressed in traditional temple costume. By evening hundreds of thousands of people have gathered on the normally deserted shore near Sanur, across from Nusa Penida.

As many as a thousand Barong are present here at the kelod extreme of the island. The marchers and their protective figures form a mighty barrier at the edge of the sea, walling out the buta, if only temporarily. And here at the edge of the ocean our account of the traditional dance of Bali is complete; from the inner court of the Berutuk temple in Trunyan to the beach at Sanur—we have come from kaja to kelod.

1. Mead (1939).
2. Laufer (1923), pp. 29–30.
3. See Pigeaud (1938), *passim*.
4. Suleiman (1974), p. 41.
5. Geertz (1963), pp. 82–141.
6. Jacobs (1883), p. 109.
7. Compare Belo (1960).
8. Liefrinck (1886), pp. 1235–7.
9. McPhee (1946), pp. 138–52, describes circumstances that called for Wayang Calonarang and other exorcist measures, as well as the performance of the shadow-play. See also Sumandhi (1979).
10. Belo (1949).
11. Hooykaas (1971).
12. Poerbatjaraka (1926), p. 152.
13. Stutterheim (1935), p. 14.
14. Holt (1967), p. 288.

Epilogue: Some Performances for Tourists

ALREADY in the nineteenth century Bali had seen the emergence of professional companies of dancers, all from the same banjar, who travelled to other villages to perform for hire at Odalan and other festivals. It was therefore no innovation when troupes of dancers and musicians were first engaged during the 1920s to perform for tourists at the Bali Hotel in Denpasar and at the hotel built by the Dutch in Kintamani village above Lake Batur.

In the second and third decades of this century, the well-known expatriate painter, Walter Spies, and other long-term European residents who came to live in the newly-discovered 'island paradise' also commissioned a large number of performances in particular villages where they had personal contacts. The companies they hired gained much-needed revenue from these engagements, while at the same time the European and American visitors were given reliable access to Balinese dance and music, without inconvenience from the vagaries of the complicated Balinese calendar of festivals.

In the 1930s the trickle of visitors became a steady flow; halted for a time by the Second World War, the stream resumed and gained momentum in the post-War era. Since 1966, when the modern Bali Beach Hotel was opened, the influx of visitors has grown to flood proportions: by 1980, one million visitors a year are expected. The dance could not remain unaffected by the inundation.[1]

In the 1930s new creations and adaptations of traditional art forms of all kinds were devised in response to the tastes of the tourist market. The art shop came into being at this time, and objects previously made to order by craftsmen were now mass-produced for sale to foreigners. Copies of sacred objects were much in demand and were provided in quantity for sale.

A similar process occurred in the dance. Various wali forms, as well as some of the secular genres, came to be performed in some villages on an almost daily basis, without regard for the calendar of religious festivals. Under the circumstances such performances could not remain truly sacred for very long. Too much is required in the way of offerings and special preparations for an authentic ceremony to be given so frequently and

[145]

without relation to the religious calendar of the people. Furthermore the traditional forms contain a great deal which is unintelligible to the foreigner.

New composite genres were developed to answer the need for an easily-understood, fast-moving, hour-long performance which did not require the use of actual sacralia. These 'imitation' traditional forms have taken on a life and place of their own in the spectrum of Balinese performance and have been to some extent authenticated through constant repetition. Although the Balinese popular audience seldom attends these mass-produced performances, they have taken on a very important economic role in the life of many villages and hence have become vital to Balinese life. After all, a tourist performance may be given one hundred times as often as the 'authentic' prototype.[2]

Cak

One such new form is *Cak*, or *Kecak*, which is sometimes called the 'Monkey Dance'. This composite genre was first created by dancers in Bedulu village, Gianyar Province, who were commissioned by Walter Spies. The group was requested to devise a new kind of *Ramayana* performance, accompanied solely by the Cak chorus found in Sang Hyang Dedari. In that old exorcist rite the choral group consists of perhaps a dozen men, each making a distinctive '*chek chek chek*' sound that blends into a complex rhythmic pattern to assist the dancers to sustain their trance condition.

This wali nucleus, much developed, is the basis for Cak, which is a purely secular performance given only for tourists. It is not usually presented in the context of village life. The first simple version created in Bedulu was instantly successful and rapidly became very popular with tourists and other visitors to Bali. Today fourteen professional groups perform regularly at the larger hotels and on special stages built for the purpose in their banjar. Tourists come in busloads on a daily basis to see the show.

In Cak the chorus of chanting men has been enlarged to a hundred or more chanters/dancers, who sit in concentric rings around a small oil-lamp. One of the members serves as the leader. Instead of simple repetitive continuous chanting, the chorus performs a highly-structured piece of vocal music, which is exactly one hour long. Melodies and musical ideas from the modern Balinese concert repertoire are heard, and the influence of the Kebyar musical style is apparent.

The creators of Cak introduced a dramatic episode into the performance, performed by a small number of skilled dancers in simple costumes. The *Ramayana* was the source, and the first story to be given was the episode of the abduction of Sita. This was a very simple representation. Later a battle sequence was added, pitting Sugriwa against Rawana's son, Indrajit. This and subsequent innovations were devised first in one village and then were quickly copied by the others, as more and more Cak groups came into being. Balinese choreographers and musicians are very alert to the efforts of their colleagues and rivals, and a successful local novelty can become standard practice all over the island in a matter of months.

In 1965 the very popular Sendratari Ramayana was introduced at KOKAR, and in 1969 students returning to Singapadu from Denpasar at the conclusion of their studies made great changes to the local Cak performance which were widely imitated. At that time the single *Ramayana* episode was lengthened to represent the whole epic tale, from the banishment of Rama to the death of Rawana. The Sendratari costumes were brought into use, and a great deal of new music from the Sendratari repertoire was adapted for the huge chorus. These innovations were adopted almost everywhere within a few months under pressure from the travel agents, who threatened to halt the buses to villages refusing to adapt their play to the newer style.

Barong and Rangda

Of all the forms of Balinese dance which interested early Western visitors and residents, the Barong, the Rangda, and the genres involving trance possession were the most fascinating. In the early 1930s, Walter Spies directed many visitors to the villages of Pagutan and Tegal Tamu in the Batubulan area, where variants of the Calonarang dance-drama were performed. In this area followers of the Barong frequently practised self-stabbing during the performance, to the great interest of scholars and curiosity seekers alike. Many special performances were commissioned by Walter Spies and his guests, and in Pagutan especially performing Calonarang became something of a local industry; three or more performances might often be requested in a single week.

With the resumption of tourism in 1948, the Bali Hotel in Denpasar requested that a Barong performance be created especially to suit the needs of the tourist trade. At that time a group of traditional artists established the form as it is seen by the tourist today. Carefully edited and tailored to fit exactly into a one-hour performance, the show is given with unconsecrated masks and with only a minimal offering to protect the dancers. No one actually goes into a trance in the performance, and sacred objects are not employed. The company is made up of members of the banjar, who divide the profits monthly, after setting aside 40 per cent for the general fund.

Although the performance is based on a *Mahabharata* story called 'Sudamala' or 'Kunti Sraya', the masks and general format are taken over from the Calonarang performance we have described. In this plot, which has been standardized so that a synopsis can be distributed to the audience, two Rangda masks are employed, worn by the goddess Durga and by her servant-priestess Kalika. When the Barong appears at the end of the play, his followers practise simulated self-stabbing and other trance-like behaviour according to a precise timetable. After the tourists depart the traditional life of the village resumes.

Prembon Concert

The term 'prembon' was originally applied to the dance-drama made up of elements from a number of separate genres, but this term has now come to refer also to a revue-style presentation first given at the Bali Beach Hotel. The permanent performing space at this modern international facility is located as close to the Sanur beach as it can be placed, and it is thus in the most kelod location of Bali. The dancers have their backs to the sea when they step onto the permanent stage, placed outdoors by the swimming pool under waving coconut palms. Imitation shrines conceal the spotlights. The stage is not consecrated.

The concert consists of half a dozen pieces, all of them like the introductory dances of Topeng in type. No dialogue or story features are included. Panyembrama is always first, usually followed by Kebyar Duduk, Legong (much abbreviated), solo Baris, Jauk, Panji Semirang, and a single Topeng mask. To the Balinese audience this is akin to a meal consisting entirely of appetizers.

The tourist performances have obviously yielded both benefits and liabilities to the artists of Bali. Among the positive effects must be noted the contribution that income from tourist performances has made to the organizations of dancers and musicians. The clubs (and the individual banjar from which its members are drawn) have been able to benefit from the purchase of new gamelan, new costumes, and so on, and these expensive items are regularly used for traditional performances given in the village context for Balinese audiences. The Bali Museum in Denpasar was also founded under the stimulus of the tourist trade, and this institution maintains an active preservation programme concerned with the support of the performing arts as well as painting, sculpture, and the traditional crafts.

On the negative side of the ledger, it is easy to see that endless repetition of performances for audiences composed entirely of people who are experiencing Balinese dance and theatre for the first time has led in many cases to a deterioration of the standards of excellence. Each of the standard types of show for tourists has already been given over and over in identical form for more than a decade, leading to some performances that seem quite stale.

[149]

The tourist is by definition a curiosity seeker in search of new sensations. Since the more exotic and (to the Westerner) sensational forms of Balinese dance are in the wali category, there has been a steady pressure, growing over time, to exhibit sacred dances for commercial purposes. This trend has been resisted by Balinese religious, cultural, and political leaders, especially since a seminar held in 1971 on the subject 'Sacred and Secular Art'. At that time I Gusti Bagus Sugriwa, the well-known expert on traditional Balinese religion and culture, proposed the basic three-part set of categories of sacred performance which we have followed in this volume. It was the conclusion of the seminar that the wali and bebali genres should not be exploited for commercial gain.[3]

But still the pressures have been intense. We might mention the Sang Hyang Dedari performance given at Bona, in which the little girls are put into trance twice a week strictly for the tourist audience; in that village the Legong has been added to make a more interesting show. And in 1977, amid great controversy, a Baris Gedé troupe from Sebatu village performed a number of wali dances for audiences in Europe and America. Since no sacred objects were employed, in the eyes of many Balinese dancers no great harm was done, although some regretted that the quality of the Sebatu performance left something to be desired.

In closing this volume we should mention briefly the discothèque lounge in the basement of the Bali Hyatt Hotel in Sanur, constructed in 1974. No performing place in Bali is lower or closer to the sea. Here visitors from all over the world—as well as Western-oriented young Balinese—dance the latest international rock and disco crazes: the *Funky Chicken*, the *Latin Hustle*, the *L.A. Bus Stop*. The resemblance to the dancing described in the old Calonarang is not too far-fetched:

> . . . Gandi danced while jumping up and down, and her hair hung to one side. Her eyes were red as a mangosteen. Lende danced on tip-toe; her face glowed like fire and her hair hung loose. Woksirsa danced pecking like a chicken while staring blankly. Her hair was loose and she was naked. Mahisawadana

[150]

danced hopping on one foot—then she turned upside down and stuck out her tongue, licking. Her hands clutched as if to capture her prey.

1. Hanna (1976), pp. xi−xiii; pp. 92−128.
2. Black and Hoefer, *Guide to Bali* (1970) is an excellent guide to 'tourist' Bali.
3. *Proyek Pemeliharaan* (1971) is the report issued at the conclusion of this seminar.

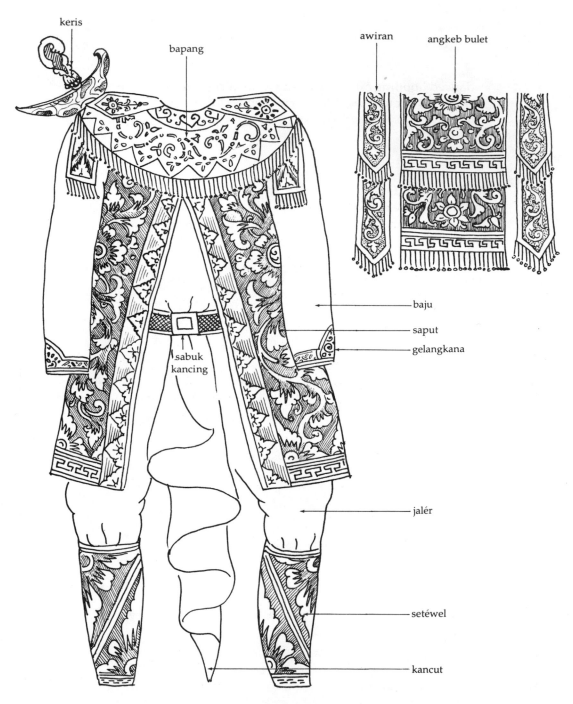

keris

bapang

awiran

angkeb bulet

baju

saput

gelangkana

sabuk
kancing

jalér

setéwel

kancut

5. Typical Male Costume (for Wayang Wong) (Courtesy I Nyoman Mandra)

[152]

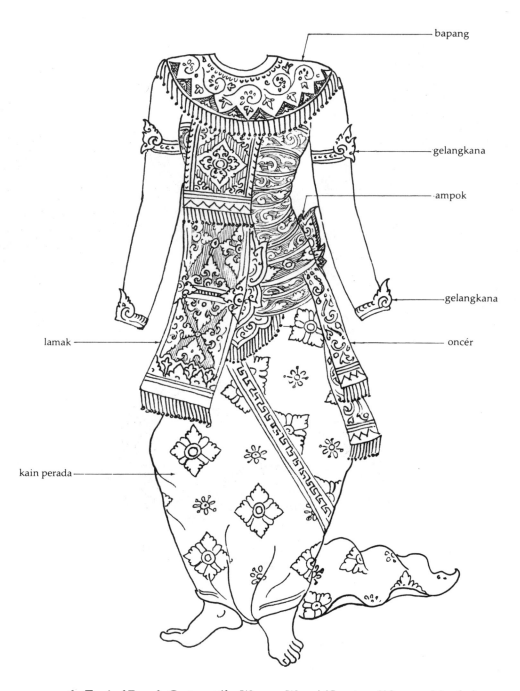

bapang

gelangkana

ampok

gelangkana

lamak

oncér

kain perada

6. Typical Female Costume (for Wayang Wong) (Courtesy I Nyoman Mandra)

[153]

Gelungan

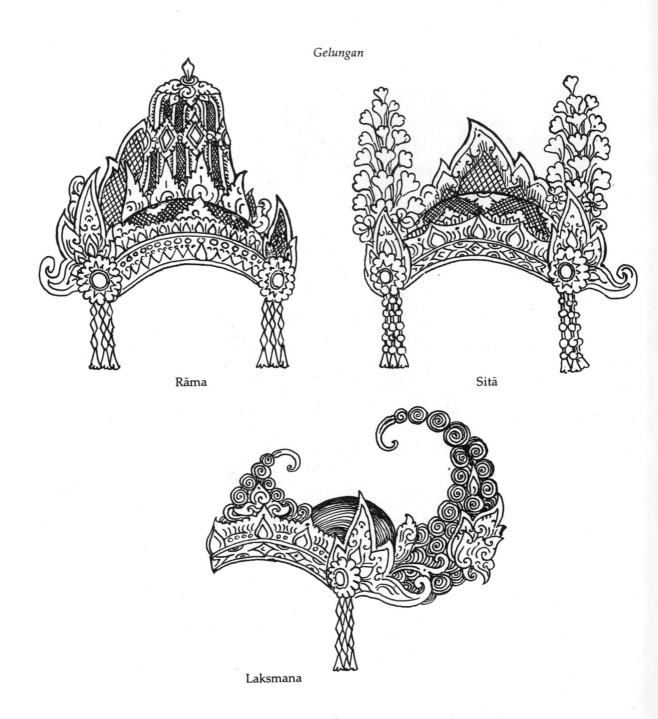

Rāma

Sitā

Laksmana

7. Typical Head-dresses (Courtesy I Nyoman Mandra)

Sugriwa

Wibisana

Delem

Twalen

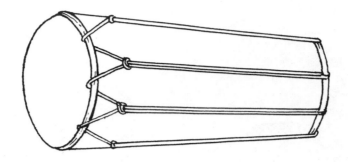

Kendang

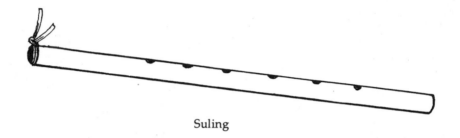

Suling

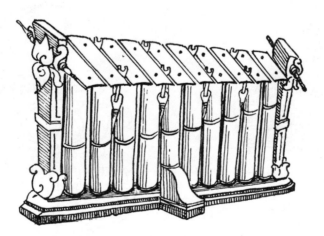

Gender Wayang

8. Some Typical Instruments (Courtesy I Nyoman Mandra)

Glossary

List of Abbreviations

C = Costume element.

D = Choreographic element; only a few of the more than eight hundred named poses, gestures, locomotive and transitional movements are listed.

G = Genre.

L = Literary source or other written work.

M = Musical term.

R = Role or character type.

S = Term applying to stage or properties.

Abuang Kalah:	(G) Old social dance ritual performed in Tenganan, a Bali Aga village.
Adar:	(G) Joged dance of the Tabanan region, now extinct.
agem:	(D) Pose or basic standing position, of various types.
agung:	Great or large.
alus:	Refined, soft or delicate.
ampok:	(C) Carved and gilded leather waistband, part of certain female costumes.
ampok bulet:	(C) Decorative cloth panel, worn at the back.
angsel:	(D & M) An abrupt rhythmic pattern of syncopated accents executed simultaneously by dancer and orchestra, culminating in a sudden pause which suspends music and dance at a definite point in the musical cycle.
anteng:	(C) Type of sash.
arak:	Rice brandy.
Arja:	(G) Very popular type of dance-drama in which the dialogue is sung; it is also known as 'Balinese opera'.

[157]

Arjuna Wiwaha:	(L) Well-known classic of Old Javanese literature, a poem of the kakawin type, used as subject for Wayang Kulit and dance-drama. It is based loosely on an episode in the Indian *Mahabharata*.
arya-arya:	(R) Four dancers representing the common soldiers in the army of Prince Panji in Gambuh.
ASTI-Bali:	Government-sponsored undergraduate dance academy located in Denpasar.
awiran:	(C) Apron simulating monkey fur, worn in Wayang Wong.
babad:	(L) Balinese historical/genealogical chronicles, devoted ordinarily to a single lineage; these accounts form the basis for the Topeng repertoire.
Babad Blahbatuh:	(L) Chronicle of the Jelantik family.
Babad Dalem:	(L) Chronicle of the family of the Kings of Klungkung, which was nominally the highest-ranked of the Balinese principalities in the pre-Colonial period.
babi guling:	Roast pork, well-loved culinary delicacy of the Balinese people.
baju:	(C) Jacket.
balé:	(S) Hall or pavilion.
balé agung:	Great hall or council house.
balé banjar:	Hall belonging to the ward association.
Bali Aga:	People considered by the Balinese to be the original inhabitants of the island. Living in certain more or less remote villages, Bali Aga people differ from their more 'Javanized' neighbours with respect to burial practices, composition of the priesthood, etc.

balian: Medicine man, ritual expert, sometimes a medium.

bali-balihan: Dance performances presented purely for the entertainment of the audience are assigned to this category.

Banaspati Raja: (R) A title given to the Barong Ket meaning 'King of the Woods'.

banchih: Neuter or bisexual; the term refers to those modern Kebyar compositions which may be performed by either male or female performers.

bandrangan: (S) Decorative lance which serves as part of the furnishings of the traditional kalangan.

banjar: Ward of a village or larger settlement.

bapang: (C) Decorative neckband or collar; also (M) title of a composition used to accompany dancing by the clowns.

Baris: (G) A group of warrior dances for males, based on military drill manoeuvres; in almost all of the Baris dances a characteristic pointed helmet is part of the costume.

Baris Bedil: (G) A type of sacred Baris dance in which the dancers carry muskets.

Baris Dadap: (G) A type of sacred Baris dance in which the dancers carry wedge-shaped shields.

Baris Gedé: (G) 'Great Baris', a type of dance done by a large group carrying spears.

Baris Melampahan: (G) Secular variety of Baris in which a drama is presented with Baris dancers in one or more of the leading roles.

Baris Panah: (G) A type of sacred Baris in which the dancers carry bows and arrows.

Baris Pendet: (G) A type of sacred Baris dance in which the dancers carry ritual vessels filled with flower petals.

Baris Tamiang:	(G) A type of sacred Baris dance in which the dancers carry shields provided with spikes in the middle.
Baris Tumbak:	(G) Another name for Baris Gedé.
Barong:	General term for a mask representing an animal or supernatural being; masks of this type have costume elements attached and cover at least the head and shoulders of the bearer. Often they are animated by two dancers, one behind the other.
Barong Asu:	(G) Barong in the shape of a giant dog.
Barong Bangkal:	(G) Barong in the shape of a fabulous wild boar.
Barong Gadjah:	(G) Barong in the shape of a great elephant.
Barong Keding-kling:	(G) Old wali genre associated with Wayang Wong; the masks, representing monkeys, are worn by male performers.
Barong Keket:	(G) Also known as Barong Ket, the best known type of Barong, resembling a dragon-like lion.
Barong Landung:	(G) A kind of giant effigy figure representing a human character; each mask is manipulated by a single performer.
Barong Lembu:	(G) Barong in the shape of a cow.
Barong Machan:	(G) Barong in the shape of a great tiger.
Barong Sai:	Not a mask but a type of lion statue in Chinese style, found on the gates of some temples.
Basur:	(L) Old Balinese tale about a sorcerer; it is the source for a dance-drama similar to the Calonarang play in which the Rangda mask is used to represent the central character when he is at the height of his magical powers.

[160]

batel: (M) Cyclical musical piece, played to accompany battle scenes and other scenes of vigorous action.

batel gender wayang: (M) Musical ensemble used to accompany Wayang Wong and Wayang Kulit *Ramayana*; it consists of a gender wayang quartet, augmented with rhythm and punctuating instruments.

bebali: Category of semi-sacred, or ceremonial, dances which are properly performed in the *jaba tengah*.

Bebali Sidhakarya: (L) Manuscript containing the lore, rules, prayers and special prescriptions applying to the performer of Topeng Pajegan.

bebona-ngan: (M) Ensemble like a marching band used to accompany processions.

belas-belasan: Going in separate directions.

Berutuk: (G) Traditional masked dance ritual performed in the Bali Aga village of Trunyan.

bondres: (R) Any of a number of comic and eccentric characters belonging to the lowest (*jaba*) caste.

brahmana: The highest-ranked, priestly, caste.

Bratayuda: (L) Twelfth century poem in Old Javanese of the kakawin type which recounts the story of the great war between the Kurawas and the Pandawas from the Indian *Mahabharata* epic. The poem is the source for episodes represented in Parwa and Wayang Kulit and is an important source of quotations sung as lyrics in various genres of dance-drama.

brem: Rice wine.

buta: Demonic spirit.

Cak: (G) The 'monkey dance', a popular form of tourist performance. Also (M) the male chorus which provides accompaniment for some of the Sang Hyang dances.

Cakapung: (G) All-male improvisatory dancing and poetry-reading party popular in Karangasem Province.

Calo-narang: (L) Old Javanese prose work, telling the story of the Widow of Girah, a witch, who is defeated by the great sage, Mpu Bharadah; a second section tells of a visit by the sage to Bali in which he crosses the ocean riding on a leaf. Episodes from the first section form the basis for Wayang Calonarang and the Calonarang dance-drama.

candi bentar: (S) Open archway in the temple wall, used by the dancers as the principal entrance or exit. Gateways of this type are also found on some secular buildings. The design is made to look as if the two sides of the gateway had been split apart down the middle.

candi kurung: (S) Covered doorway, also used as an entrance and exit by dancers.

capung mandus: (D) Movement resembling a dragonfly playing by the water.

caru: Offering placed on the ground to placate *buta*.

Cokorda: Feudal title applied to the highest members of the Ksatrya caste. The Cokorda was the reigning monarch.

Condong: (C) The maidservant, a type character resembling the soubrette in Western tradition; she interprets the Kawi and High Balinese of her mistress in many genres.

Cupak and Grantang: (L) Balinese story telling of a pair of brothers, one virtuous and handsome, the other ugly and gluttonous but highly *sakti*. The story, sometimes embellished with motifs from the Calonarang play, is presented in various genres such as Janger and Wayang Kulit.

daag: (R) Formerly, the master of ceremonies at the Janger performance.

dalang: Shadow puppeteer. A literary expert, the dalang often serves as dramaturg and choreographer.

dalem: Deep, majestic, inner.

Dalem: (R) King of the good party in Topeng.

dedari: (R) From the Sanskrit *vidyadhari*, the heavenly nymphs of Hindu mythology.

Delem: (R) Chief *penasar* to the antagonist party (the villain) in Wayang Kulit, Wayang Wong, and Parwa. Pompous and ridiculous, Delem is very popular with the audience.

Demang: (R) Prince Panji's Prime Minister and Commander of the Armed Forces in Gambuh.

desa: Village.

desa adat: Traditional village government.

dewa, dewi: God, goddess.

Dewagung: Title for the highest ranking King.

Dharmaning Sangging: (L) Manuscript containing the lore, prayers, rituals, and special prescriptions applying to the maker of sacred masks.

Drama Gong: (G) Modern theatrical form, a descendant of Stambul. Lacking in choreographic features, the drama is accompanied by one of the gamelan gong ensembles.

dukun: Folk doctor, sometimes a magician.

dusang: Corpse.

Dusang: (R) The person who portrays the corpse of one of the widow's victims in the Calonarang dance-drama.

engotan: (D) Movement common in many genres in which the head is shifted quickly from side to side

Gabor: (G) Ritual dance for females in which offerings are presented.

Galuh: (R) The heroine in Arja.

Galungan: Major Balinese religious holiday, lasting for ten days; it is the occasion for countless performances all over the island.

Gambuh: (G) 'Expert', the oldest surviving form of dance-drama. Belonging to the bebali group, it is considered to be the source of all Balinese dramatic dance.

gambuh suling: (M) Long endblown flute which is played with a difficult circular breathing technique; it is the main instrument of the gamelan gambuh.

gamelan: (M) Any Balinese orchestral ensemble which includes rhythmic and punctuating instruments. There are many different types.

gamelan batel: (M) See batel gender wayang.

gamelan gambuh: (M) Ensemble which accompanies the Gambuh dance-drama; it consists of four gambuh suling plus drums, other percussion instruments, and gongs.

gamelan gong: (M) Traditional large orchestral ensemble, used to accompany Topeng and other dance genres. There are a number of types.

gamelan gong gedé: (M) The largest traditional orchestral ensemble of Bali, now very rarely found.

gamelan gong kebyar: (M) Large modern instrumental ensemble, used to accompany the Kebyar genres, as well as for purely musical compositions.

gamelan semar peguli-ngan: (M) Also known as gamelan pelegongan, this traditional orchestral ensemble, once reserved for nobility, is associated with amorous dalliance. It accompanied certain Joged and Gandrung dances, as well as Legong.

Gandrung: (G) Dance of the Joged group performed by young boys rather than girls.

[164]

Gebyog: (G) Social dance related to Joged, formerly performed improvisationally during the rice harvest.

gedé: Large, great.

gelang-kana: (C) Wristband.

gelatik nuwut papah: (D) Movement resembling a bird jumping sideways along a tree branch.

gelung: (C) Head-dress—there are many types. Often gelung have or acquire sacral qualities, especially in unmasked genres such as Gambuh.

gender wayang quartet: (M) Small instrumental ensemble composed of four gender, an instrument having ten tuned bronze keys suspended over resonating tubes. It is played with a difficult two-handed technique to accompany Wayang Kulit.

genggong: (M) Instrument resembling the Jew's harp.

Godogan: (G) Balinese folk-tale that has been made into a modern dance-drama; the story is a variant of the well-known tale of the Princess who marries a frog.

gongsor: (C) Ornament resembling a necktie, usually made from feathers.

Hari Raya Nyepi: The Balinese New Year's holiday.

ibing: Male dancer (usually amateur) who comes from the audience to dance with the performer in Joged dances.

idep: Thought, belief.

igel: Dance.

igel ngugal: Section of a scene in a dance-drama in which an important character is introduced; it may be long or short in duration, depending on the character and the place of the scene in the structure of the

[165]

	drama as a whole. After the igel ngugal the dramatic action may begin.
igel pajeng:	Section of a dance composition in which the performer dances with an umbrella.
igel sambir:	Section of a dance composition in which movement involving the sambir is featured.
jaba:	Outside; the third temple courtyard; the lowest caste, to which the great majority of Balinese people belong.
jaba tengah:	The second temple courtyard, ante-room to the jeroan.
jaler:	(C) White trousers, part of the male costume.
Janger:	(G) Twentieth-century genre in which elements from many sources are combined; circus stunts and military drill are characteristic elements of the performance.
Jauk:	(G) Masked dance presenting a demonic character in which a particular stupa-shaped conical helmet is worn.
Jayaprana:	(L) Balinese romantic story, a popular subject for Sendratari.
jeroan:	The inner courtyard of the temple, its most sacred precinct.
Jeru Gedé:	(R) 'Large Person', the father in Barong Landung.
Jeru Luh:	(R) 'Female Person', the mother in Barong Landung.
Joged:	(G) A group of dances in which the performers dance sequentially with men from the audience (ibing) who improvise flirtatiously.
Joged Bumbung:	(G) Formerly popular modern type of Joged accompanied by an ensemble featuring bamboo (bumbung) xylophones.
Joged Gudegan:	(G) Joged genre. Also known as Joged Pingitan or Joged Tongkohan.

juru tandak:	(M) The principal male singer; he sits in the gamelan and provides narration and even dialogue for the dancers in some genres, such as Legong and Sendratari.
kade-kadehan:	(R) Heralds in the court of Prabu in Gambuh.
kain perada:	(C) Wraparound skirt made of gilded cloth, part of female costume.
kain poleng:	(C & S) Checkered cloth used for flags, banners, and for various costume elements, thought to have beneficial magical properties.
kaja:	Direction toward the north, high, holy, central in an old Balinese system of orientation.
kakan-kakan:	(R) Female retainers attending the Putri in Gambuh.
kakawin:	Poem in the Old Javanese language composed according to Sanskrit metrical principles. Quotations from the most venerated kakawins such as the *Ramayana* and *Arjuna Wiwaha* are used as lyric by the dancers and the stories told in the old poems are favourite subjects in the dramatic repertoire.
kalangan:	(S) The traditional Balinese arena stage.
kasar:	Coarse, rough, vulgar.
Kawi:	The Old Javanese language, ancestral language of the Balinese people; it is spoken by the important characters of high rank in Wayang Kulit and in many genres of dance-drama.
kebaya:	(C) Traditional Indonesian blouse.
Kebyar:	(G) 'Lightning', the popular modern Balinese dance genre and musical style.
Kebyar bebancihan:	'Neuter' Kebyar, or Kebyar dances that may be performed by male and female performers alike.
Kebyar	(G) 'Sitting Kebyar', a dance in the popular style

Duduk: created by the great I Mario of Tabanan; the dancer performs in a squatting position.

kecak: Male semi-chorus in Janger.

Kecak: Name given occasionally to the Cak dance.

keker: Forest cock, complement to the kiuh.

kelod: Direction toward the south, low, demonic, periphery in an old Balinese system of orientation.

kendhang: (M) Drum.

kepeng: Chinese coin with a hole in the centre, once the basic unit of Balinese currency.

keras: Strong, rough, forceful.

kerawuhan: In a state of trance.

keris: Traditional Balinese dagger.

kidang rebut muring: (D) Movement resembling the jumping of a deer pestered by biting flies.

kidung: (L) Poem in the Old Javanese language following Indonesian metrical principles. Also (M) a style of singing associated with such texts.

kiuh: Forest fowl, complement to the keker.

ksatrya: Knightly caste from which Bali's feudal rulers were drawn.

kul-kul: (M) Large wooden slit-drum.

lamak: (C) Decorative apron, part of the female costume.

langsé: (S) Decoratively painted front curtain.

Legong: (G) Classical dance genre, semi-dramatic in nature, performed by two or three young girls between ten and twelve years of age.

Leko: (G) Genre of the Joged group.

leyak: Demon or familiar spirit.

Limbur: (R) Comic matron, a popular stock character in Arja.

lontar:	Balinese palm-leaf manuscript.
mabasan:	Ceremonial oral chanting and interpretation of the Balinese literary classics.
Maha-bharata:	(L) Indian epic poem, source for much of the Balinese dramatic repertoire, known in Bali principally through the medium of Old Javanese works such as the *Bratayuda*, the *Parwas*, and adaptations like *Arjuna Wiwaha*.
Malat:	(L) Old Indonesian epic poem, the source of the Panji story as it is represented in Gambuh, Legong, Arja, and elsewhere in Balinese dance.
manis:	Sweet, refined, gentle.
Matah Gedé:	(R) 'The Great Uncooked One', a name applied to the Widow of Girah in the Calonarang dance-drama, as she appears before she transforms into the Rangda.
mawinten:	Artist's consecration ceremony.
medagang:	'Selling', the process of bargaining employed in former times by certain joged, gandrung, and penyeroan.
Memendet:	(G) Ritual dance, counterpart to Gabor, performed by priests or male members of the congregation.
mengigel:	To dance.
Merga-pati:	(G) Dance belonging to the Kebyar group in which a character study is presented.
mudra:	(D) Sacred hand poses and gestures employed by priests in their rituals and in certain dances.
mungkah lawang:	(D) Movement involved in opening the front curtain (langsé). When no curtain is actually present the gesture symbolizes the beginning.
nadab gelung:	(D) Touching the head-dress with a particular gesture.
nadi:	In a state of trance (from 'dadi', to become).

[169]

Nandir: (G) Classical dance genre similar to Legong, performed by young boys.

ngelawang: To go 'on the road' with the Barong at the time of the Galungan holiday.

ngelayak: (D) Bending movement resembling a tree bowing under the weight of many flowers.

ngibing: To dance as an ibing.

ngurek: Ritual self-stabbing, done with keris or other weapon.

odalan: Calendrical temple festival.

onying: Another word for ngurek.

padma-sana: Stone shrine for the gods of the Hindu trinity.

pajegan: As a whole, refers to the Topeng performance in which a soloist performs all the roles.

pajeng: (S) Umbrella.

pamurtian: (R) Powerful and wrathful manifestation which certain demonic and divine characters have the power to assume.

Pandung: (R) Patih in the Calonarang dance-drama.

pangkat: Formal exit or departure sequence.

Panji: (R) Refined hero in Gambuh.

Panji Semirang: (G) Kebyar dance portraying Princess Candra Kirana, refined heroine of the Panji story as told in Malat.

pantun: Indonesian song style in which semi-choruses sing back and forth in question and answer format.

Panyem-brama: (G) Recently-created welcoming dance, based on Rejang.

parekan: (R) Servants, retainers.

parta-pukan: Old Javanese word for masked dancer.

Parwa: (G) Dance-drama like Wayang Wong based on the *Mahabharata*.

the Parwas: (L) Old Javanese prose works, more or less faithful translations of certain chapters from the *Mahabharata*.

pasupati: Magical power.

Patih: Prime Minister and Commander of the Armed Forces, a strong character found in many genres; a Patih may belong to either party in the drama.

pedanda: Priest belonging to the brahmana caste.

pegunem: Audience or meeting scene.

pekaad: Final section of the Legong dance.

pelinggih: Shrine.

pelog: (M) Tuning system in which successive intervals between the pitches vary greatly. In its most complete form it consists of seven tones within the octave, but in modern practice five tone scales are drawn from the seven, with the omitted tones serving only as passing or substitute tones.

pemangku: Lower-caste priest.

penasar: (R) Clown or buffoon characters who serve as attendants to the leading male characters; they interpret the Kawi spoken by their masters and add comic relief.

Penasar Cenikan: (R) The sly younger penasar in Topeng.

Penasar Kelihan: (R) The pompous older penasar in Topeng.

pengarti: 'Explainer', in Cakapung the performer who interprets the chanted poetry.

pengawak: 'Body', the main section of the dance composition.

pengawit: Opening or prologue section of the dance composition.

[171]

pengecet:	Final section of the dance composition.
penge-lembar:	Introductory series of masks in Topeng.
pengipuk:	Courtship scene.
penudusan:	'Smoking' the Sang Hyang or other ritual dancers to assist them in entering a trance state.
penyeroan:	Prostitute.
penyor:	(S) Decorative flag-like banner.
pesiat:	Battle scene.
pinggel:	(C) Arm band.
pingit:	Secret, sacred.
pohon kepuh:	Graveyard tree. (Also known as pohon rangdu.)
Potet:	(R) Comic group of soldiers led by Prabangsa in Gambuh.
Prabangsa:	(R) Chief minister to Prabu in Gambuh; prototype of the strong rough Patih.
Prabu:	(R) Antagonist King, or 'villain', in Gambuh.
pratima:	Wooden effigies into which the deities descend at an odalan.
Prembon:	(G) Dance-drama created by combining stock elements from several different genres. Also, recently, a revue made up of short pieces from different genres.
punggawa:	Village headman.
pura:	Temple.
pura dalem:	Sometimes called the 'death temple', the pura dalem is one of three temples maintained in most villages; it is considered to be the dwelling of the god Ciwa.
pura desa:	Village temple dedicated to Wisnu.
Pura Peng-rebongan:	'Meeting Temple', a place of worship sacred to Barong and Rangda masks.

pura puseh:	'Origin temple', the village temple sacred to the god Brahma.
puri:	Palace.
Putri:	(R) Heroine of the Gambuh performance, the Princess. She is the prototype for refined female characters in more recent genres.
rajeg:	(S) Spear or lance.
Ramayana:	(L) Indian epic poem, known in Bali by means of an Old Javanese kakawin. It is frequently recited by mabasan groups and forms the basis for the repertoire of Wayang Wong, Wayang Kulit Ramayana, Cak, Sendratari, and, to an extent, Barong Kedingkling.
Rangda:	(R) 'The Widow', a mask of demonic aspect named for the Widow of Girah, Calonarang. In fact the Widow is only one of a number of characters which may be represented by means of this mask.
rangki:	(S) Dressing and retiring room for the dancers.
Ratu Dalem:	'Monarch of the Temple', a name given to the Rangda mask.
Ratu Desa:	'Monarch of the Village', a name given to the Rangda mask.
Ratu Pancering Jagat:	'God Navel of the World', object of devotion in Trunyan, a Bali Aga village.
rebana:	(M) Single-headed Arab drum.
Rejang:	(G) Ancient temple dance for women.
ronggeng:	Public dancing girl, joged. (Also known as joged tongkohan.)
rumbing:	(C) Ear ornament.
sabda:	The word, language.
sabuk kancing:	(C) Belt.

sakti: Supernaturally powerful.

sambir: (C) Cape-like skirt wrapped and tied below the armpits which forms the lower part of certain male costumes.

sang hyang: Protective divinity.

Sang Hyang: (G) A group of exorcistic dances involving spirit possession.

Sang Hyang Celeng: (G) Sang Hyang dance in which the performer is possessed by a pig spirit.

Sang Hyang Dedari: (G) Sang Hyang dance in which the performers are possessed by the spirits of celestial nymphs.

Sang Hyang Jaran: (G) Sang Hyang dance in which the performers are possessed by a horse spirit.

Sang Hyang Legong: (G) Ritual Legong genre.

sanggah: Family temple.

sanggah taksu: Shrine dedicated to the artist's inspiration.

Sangut: (R) Younger penasar serving the antagonist party in Wayang Kulit, Wayang Wong, and Parwa. A great favourite with the audience, Sangut is more prudent and better-natured than his brother Delem.

saput: (C) Another name for sambir.

sayar-soyor: (D) Movement resembling a tree swaying in the wind.

sebel: Ritually polluted, unclean.

seka: Club or association.

seka mabasan: Club devoted to readings from literary classics.

seka taruna: Association of the young bachelors of a village.

sekar taji: (C) Winglike decorative leather collar.

seledet: (D) Eye-flicking movements.

selonding: (M) Sacred iron gamelan ensembles of great antiquity, preserved in certain old villages.

Semar:	(R) Penasar to Panji in Gambuh.
sembah:	(D) A bow with clasped hands.
Sendratari:	(G) Modern pantomimic dance-drama, perform-ed without dialogue.
setagen:	(C) Long sash.
setewel:	(C) Leggings.
Sidha Karya:	(R) Sacred mask worn as part of the ritual in Topeng Pajegan.
sisya:	Students, apprentices.
Sisya:	(R) Student witches in the Calonarang play.
slendro:	(M) Tuning system in which successive intervals between the pitches do not vary greatly. There are five tones to the octave. Ensembles in slendro tuning accompany Wayang Kulit, Wayang Wong, Parwa, Janger, and Joged Bumbung.
Stambul:	(G) Dramatic genre based in part on imitation of Western drama.
Sutri:	Temple dance similar to Rejang performed in Batuan, Gianyar Province.
taksu:	Magical power, inspiration.
tambur:	(M) Single-headed Arab drum.
tari:	Dance.
Tari Tani:	(G) 'Peasant Dance', a modern composition.
taruna:	Youth, bachelor.
telek:	(R) Also teledek, the female counterpart to the jauk; she wears a refined mask and character-istic head-dress.
tembang:	(M) Song.
tenda:	(S) Painted backdrop used in Janger.
tenget:	Sacral power.
tetam-buran:	Section of the Janger performance in which the tambur is featured.
tingga:	(S) Rangda's shack in the *Calonarang* play.

Topeng: (G) Masked dance-drama based on historical chronicles of the Balinese ruling families.

Topeng Pajegan: (G) A ritual masked dance-drama performed by a single actor-dancer-priest; he brings a dozen masks to life during the performance.

Topeng Panca: (G) 'Five-Man Topeng', a genre in which a historical tale is presented by a group of masked dancers.

Topeng Wali: (G) Another name for Topeng Pajegan, emphasizing its ritual nature.

trompong: (M) Old-fashioned instrument consisting of a row of knobbed gongs aligned in a wooden case, played by the dancer in Kebyar Duduk.

Trunajaya: (G) Dance of the Kebyar group, similar to Mergapati, Wiranata, and Yudapati.

Tua: (R) A dignified old man, frequently presented among the introductory masks in the Topeng performance.

tuak: Palm wine.

Tumeng-gung: (R) Partner to Demang, a courier in Panji's entourage in Gambuh.

Tumuli-lingan: (G) 'Bumblebee', a duet in Kebyar style created by I Mario in 1952.

tutup pala: (C) Epaulettes.

Twalen: (R) Leading penasar of the protagonist's party in Wayang Kulit, Wayang Wong, and Parwa.

uang: Money.

udeng: (C) Typical Balinese head-dress, worn by males on festive occasions.

usaba nini: Type of Balinese temple festival.

wali: Sacred. Certain dances have been classified as wali, denoting their holy status.

wantilan: (S) Cock-fight arena, often serves as an indoor secular theatre.

wayah:	Venerable, dignified.
wayang:	Shadow.
Wayang Calonarang:	(G) Sub-genre of Wayang Kulit devoted to the presentation of the *Calonarang* story, usually for exorcistic purposes.
Wayang Kulit:	(G) The shadow-puppet theatre of Bali. It is quite different in many respects from its Javanese counterpart, also called Wayang Kulit.
Wayang Kulit Ramayana:	(G) Sub-genre of Wayang Kulit devoted to the *Ramayana* repertoire; it shares many characteristics with the basic form, which presents stories based on the *Mahabharata* stories.
Wayang Lemah:	(G) Ritual shadow-puppet play, performed in the daytime without lamp or screen; the puppets are pressed against a string stretched between two dadap stalks.
Wayang Wong:	(G) Dramatic dance genre in which episodes from the *Ramayana* are presented. To some extent the masked actor-dancers imitate the movements of the puppets of the shadow theatre.
widyadari:	(R) From the Sanskrit *vidyadhari*, the heavenly nymphs of Hindu mythology.
Wiranata:	(G) Dance of the Kebyar group in which the character of a brave King is presented.
wong:	Human being.
wong sakti:	'Man of power', a specialist in dangerous ritual tasks.
Wredah:	(R) Younger retainer attending to the protagonist in Wayang Kulit, Wayang Wong and Parwa.
Wredhi Budaya:	Balinese Arts Centre, a performance space just outside Denpasar.
Yudapati:	(G) 'King of Battle', a dance of the Kebyar group depicting a King by that name.

[177]

Sources and Further Reading

Artaud, Antonin, 'On the Balinese Theater', in *The Theater and its Double*, pp. 53–67. New York: Grove Press, 1958. (French ed., 1938.)

Bandem, I Madé, 'Panji Characterization in the Gambuh Dance Drama', unpublished M.A. thesis, U.C.L.A., 1972.

———, 'Wayang Wong in Contemporary Bali', unpublished Ph.D. dissertation, Wesleyan University, 1980.

———, and deBoer, Fredrik, 'Gambuh: a Classical Balinese Drama', *Asian Music*, X–1 (1978), pp. 115–27.

Belo, Jane, *Bali: Rangda and Barong*, Monographs of the American Ethnological Society, 16, Seattle: University of Washington, 1949.

———, *Bali: Temple Festival*, American Ethnological Society Monographs, 22, Locust Valley, N.Y.: J. J. Augustin, 1953.

———, *Trance in Bali*, New York: Columbia University Press, 1960.

———, *Traditional Balinese Culture*, New York and London: Columbia University Press, 1970.

Berg, C. C., *Kidung Pamancangah; de Geschiedenis van het Rijk van Gelgel*, Singaradja and Sandpoort: Kirtya Liefrinck van de Tuuk, 1929.

Bernet-Kempers, A. J., *Ancient Indonesian Art*, Amsterdam: Van der Peet, 1959.

———, *Monumental Bali: Introduction to Balinese Archaeology: Guide to the Monuments*, The Hague: Van Goor Zonen, 1978.

Boon, James, *The Anthropological Romance of Bali 1597–1972*. Cambridge: Cambridge University Press, 1977.

Coast, John, *Dancers of Bali*, New York: Putnam, 1953.

Cool, Captain W., *With the Dutch in the East*, translated by E. J. Taylor, London: Luzac, 1897. (Dutch ed., 1896.)

Covarrubias, Miguel, *Island of Bali*. New York: Alfred Knopf, 1937; reprinted Kuala Lumpur: Oxford University Press, 1973.

deBoer, Fredrik, 'Balinese *Wayang Kulit* Ramayana', a paper presented to the Conference on Asian Puppet Theatre, School of Oriental and African Studies, London: March, 1979.

————, 'Pak Rajeg's Life in Art; Biography of a Balinese *Dalang*', *The Drama Review* T82 (June 1979), pp. 57–62.

De Kleen, Tyra, *Mudras; the Ritual Handposes of the Buddha priests and Shiva priests of Bali*, NewYork: University Books, 1970. (First published 1923.)

de Zoete, Beryl and Spies, Walter, *Dance and Drama in Bali*, London: Faber and Faber, 1938; reprinted Kuala Lumpur: Oxford University Press, 1973.

Emigh, John, 'Playing with the past; visitation and illusion in the Mask Theatre of Bali', *The Drama Review* T82 (June 1979), pp. 11–36.

Friedrich, R., *The Civilization and Culture of Bali*, Calcutta: Sisil Gupta, 1959. (1st Dutch ed., 1849–50.)

Geertz, Clifford, *Peddlers and Princes*, Chicago and London: University of Chicago, 1963.

————, *The Interpretation of Cultures*, New York: Basic Books, 1973.

Geertz, Hildred and Geertz, Clifford, *Kinship in Bali*, Chicago and London: The University of Chicago Press, 1975.

Goris, Roelof, *Prasasti Bali*, 2 vols., Bandung: Masa Baru, 1954.

Gralapp, Leland W., 'Balinese Painting and the *Wayang* Tradition', *Artibus Asia* (1967), pp. 239–66.

Hanna, Willard A., *Bali Profile; People, Events, Circumstances 1001–1976*, New York and Wheelock, N. H.: American Universities Field Staff, 1976.

Hoefer, Hans and Black, Star, *Guide to Bali*, Denpasar, Bali: Hotel Bali Beach, 1970.

Holt, Claire, *Art in Indonesia; Continuities and Change*, Ithaca, N.Y.: Cornell University Press, 1967.

Hooykaas, C., 'Pamurtian in Balinese Art', *Indonesia* 12 (October 1971), pp. 1–21.

Jacobs, Dr. Julius, *Eenigen Tijd onder de Baliers, eene Reisbeschrijving*, Batavia: G. Kolff, 1883.

Jasper, J. E., 'De "Gandroeng Bali" Fragment van een verslag in de Javabode over de tentoonstelling te Bondowoso', *Tijdschrift voor Binnenlandsche Bestuur* 23 (1902), pp. 414–18.

Kakul, I Nyoman, 'Jelantik goes to Blambangan; a *Topeng* play', translated by John Emigh and I Madé Bandem, *The Drama Review* T82 (June 1979), pp. 37–48.

Laufer, Berthold, *Oriental Theatricals*, Chicago: Field Museum of Natural History, 1923.

Liefrinck, F. A., 'De rijstcultuur op Bali', *De Indische Gids*, II (1886), pp. 1033–59, 1213–37, 1557–68.

McPhee, Colin, 'Dance in Bali', *Dance Index* VII (1948), pp. 156–208.

———, 'The Balinese Wayang Kulit and its Music', *Djawa 16* (1936), pp. 1–34. Reprinted in Jane Belo, *Traditional Balinese Culture*, New York and London: Columbia University Press, 1970, pp. 146–97.

———, *A House in Bali*, New York: John Day, 1946; reprinted Kuala Lumpur: Oxford University Press, 1979.

———, *Music in Bali*, New Haven and London: Yale University Press, 1966.

Mead, Margaret, 'The Strolling Players in the Mountains of Bali', *Natural History*, 43 (1939), pp. 137–45.

Noosten, H. H., 'Maskers en Ziekten op Java en Bali', *Djawa 16* (1936), pp. 311–17.

Pigeaud, Th., *Javaanse Volksvertoningen*, Batavia, 1938.

Poerbatjaraka, R. Ng., 'De Calon Arang', *Bijdragen tot de Taal-, Land- en Volkenkunde*, 82 (1926), pp. 110–80.

———, *Pandji-verhalen onderling vergeleken*, Bandung, 1940.

Proyek Pemeliharaan dan Pengembangan Kebudayaan Daerah Bali, *Seminar Seni Sacral dan Seni 'Profan' Bidang Tari*, Denpasar, Bali: mimeographed, 1971.

Raffles, Sir Thomas, *History of Java*, 2 vols., London, 1817. Reprinted Oxford University Press, 1965.

Ras, J. J., 'The Panji Romance and W. H. Rassers' Analysis of its Theme', *Bijdragen tot de Taal-, Land- en Volkenkunde*, 129 (1973), pp. 411–56.

Rassers, W. H., 'On the Meaning of Javanese Drama', in *Panji the Culture Hero*. The Hague: Nijhoff, 1959, pp. 1—62. (First published in Dutch, 1925.)

Robson, S. O., 'The Kawi Classics in Bali', *Bijdragen tot de Taal-, Land- en Volkenkunde*, 128 (1972), pp. 307—29.

——, *Wangbang Wedeya; A Javanese Panji Romance*, The Hague: Martinus Nijhoff, 1971.

Soekmono, R., *Pengantar Sejarah Kebudayaan Indonesia*, Jogjakarta: Penerbit Yayasan Kanisius, 1973.

Spies, Walter, 'Bericht über den Zustand von Tanz und Musik in der Negara Gianyar', *Djawa*, 16 (1936),pp. 51—9.

Spies, W. and Goris, R., 'Overzicht van Dans en Tooneel in Bali', *Djawa 17* (1937), pp. 205—27.

Stutterheim, W. F., *Indian Influences in Old Balinese Art*, London: The India Society, 1935.

Suleiman, Satyawati, *Concise Ancient History of Indonesia*. Jakarta: The Archeological Foundation, 1974.

Sumandhi, I Nyoman, *A Performance of Wayang Kulit Calonarang*, unpublished M.A. thesis, Wesleyan University, 1979.

Universitas Udayana, *Pengaruh 'Mass Tourism' terhadap Tata Kehidupan Masyarakat Bali*. Denpasar, Bali: mimeographed, 1973.

Van der Veur, Paul, 'Cultural Aspects of the Eurasian Community in Indonesian Colonial Society', *Indonesia* 6 (October, 1968), pp. 51—2.

Van Eck, R., 'Schetsen van het eiland Bali', *Tijdschrift voor Nederlandsche Indie*, new series, Vol. 9, pt. 2 (1880), pp. 14—15.

Waanders, F. L. Van Bloemen, 'Aanteekeningen omtrent de zeden en gebruiken der Balineezen, inzonderheid die van Boeleleng', *Tijdschrift van de Bataavische Genootschap van Kunsten en Wetenschap van Nederlandsche-Indie*, 3rd series, Vol. 8, pt. 2 (1859), pp. 105—279.

Zoetmulder, P. J., *Kalangwan; A Survey of Old Javanese Literature*, The Hague: Martinus Nijhoff, 1974.

Index

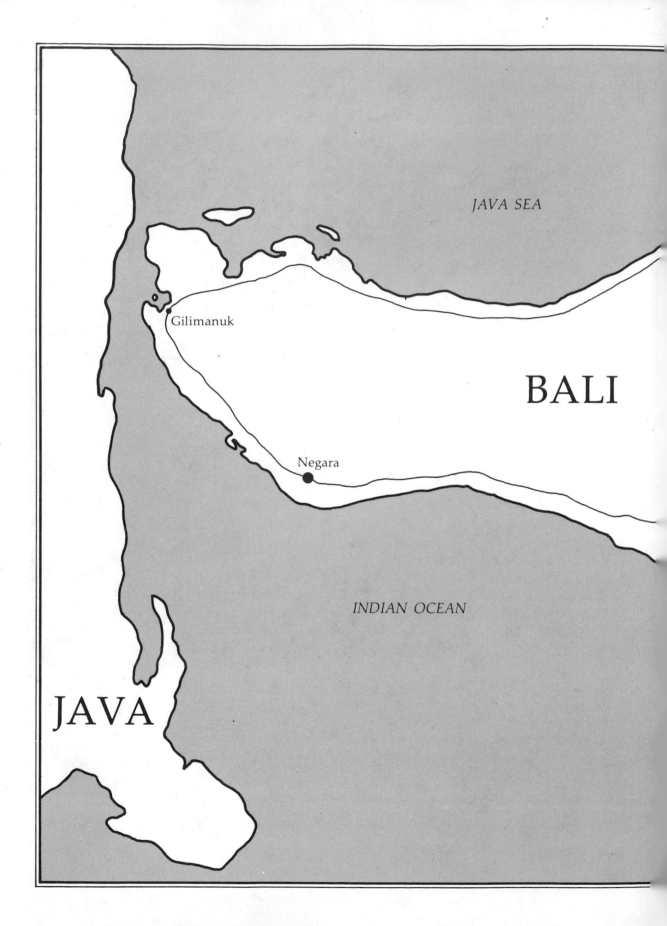

JAVA SEA

JAVA SEA

Gilimanuk

BALI

Negara

INDIAN OCEAN

JAVA